SAXOPHONE OM

For B♭ Instruments • Transcribed Exactly from Artist Recorded Solos

Songs that were originally played on E♭ instruments have been transposed for B♭ instruments.
Some notes or phrases may be out of range, and may be played an octave lower.

ISBN 978-1-5400-9303-5

Visit Hal Leonard Online at
www.halleonard.com

World headquarters, contact:
Hal Leonard
7777 West Bluemound Road
Milwaukee, WI 53213
Email: info@halleonard.com

In Europe, contact:
Hal Leonard Europe Limited
1 Red Place
London, W1K 6PL
Email: info@halleonardeurope.com

In Australia, contact:
Hal Leonard Australia Pty. Ltd.
4 Lentara Court
Cheltenham, Victoria, 3192 Australia
Email: info@halleonard.com.au

CONTENTS

ARTIST INDEX

All the Things You Are

(Booker Ervin's solo)

from *Booker Ervin: The Songbook*

Lyrics by Oscar Hammerstein II

Music by Jerome Kern

Tenor Saxophone

Medium Bop (♩ = 232)

Piano Solo

Gm6 A♭7 Gm6 A♭7

Gm6 A♭7 G7♯5 A♭7 D7

(A) **Head**

Gm7 Cm7 F7 B♭maj7 E♭maj7

Em7♭5 A7 3 Dmaj7 Dm7

Gm7 C7 Fmaj7 B♭maj7

Bm7♭5 E7 Amaj7 D6 C♯m7 C9 (B) Bm7

E7♭9 Amaj7 G♯m7 C♯9

F♯maj9 D7♯5(♯9) (C) Gm7 Cm7

F7
B♭maj7
E♭maj7
E♭m9
A♭9
Dm7
D♭dim7
Cm7
F9
B♭maj9 N.C.
D
Sax Solo
Gm7
Cm7
F7
B♭maj7
E♭maj7
Em7♭5
A7
Dmaj7
Dm7
Gm7
C7
Fmaj7
F7
B♭maj7
Bm7♭5
E7
Amaj7
D6
C♯m7
C9
E
Bm7
E7♭9
Amaj7
G♯m7
C♯9
F♯maj9

D7♯5(♯9)
F
Gm7
Cm7
F7
B♭maj7
E♭maj7
E♭m9
A♭9
Dm7
D♭dim7
Cm7
F9
B♭maj9
Am7♭5
D7
G
Gm7
Cm7
F7
B♭maj7
E♭maj7
Em7♭5
A7
Dmaj7
Dm7
Gm7
C7
Fmaj7
F7
B♭maj7
Bm7♭5
E7
Amaj7
D6
C♯m7
C9
H
Bm7
E7♭9
Amaj7

G♯m7
C♯9
F♯maj9
D7♯5(♯9)
I
Gm7
Cm7
F7
B♭maj7
E♭maj7
E♭m9
A♭9
Dm7
D♭dim7
Cm7
F9
B♭maj9
Am7♭5
D7
J
Gm7
Cm7
F7
B♭maj7
E♭maj7
Em7♭5
A7
Dmaj7
Dm7
Gm7
C7
Fmaj7
F7
B♭maj7

Bm7♭5
E7
Amaj7
3
D6
C♯m7
C9
K
Bm7
8va
E7♭9
(8va)
Amaj7
G♯m7
C♯9
(8va)
F♯maj9
D7♯5(♯9)
L
Gm7
Cm7
F7
B♭maj7
E♭maj7
E♭m9
A♭9
Dm7
D♭dim7
Cm7
F9
B♭maj9
Am7♭5
D7
M
Piano Solo
Gm7
Cm7
34
N
36
O
36
P
Head
Gm7
Cm7
F7
B♭maj7

E♭maj7
Em7♭5
A7
3
Dmaj7
Dm7
Gm7
C7
Fmaj7
F7
B♭maj7
Bm7♭5
E7
3
Amaj7
D6
C♯m7
C9
Q
Bm7
E7♭9
Amaj7
G♯m7
C♯9
F♯maj9
D7♯5(♯9)
R
Gm7
Cm7
F7
B♭maj7
E♭maj7
E♭m9
A♭9
Dm7
D♭dim7
S
Piano Solo
Cm7
3
F9
3
Gm6
A♭9
Gm6
A♭9
12
12
Fadeout...

Alone Together

(Joe Lovano's solo)

from *Joe Lovano: Joyous Encounter*

Lyrics by Howard Dietz

Music by Arthur Schwartz

C♯m7 F♯7
C7 Am7 D7♭9 G C♯9♯11
C B7♭9 Emaj7
D
Bm7♭5
E7 Am
B♭m7 E♭7
Am7 D7 Gmaj7 C♯9♯11
E
C7 B7♭9 Em C♯7♯9 F♯m7♭5 B7♭9
Em C♯m7♭5 F♯7♯9 B7♭9 Em A7

C7
B7♭13
Em11
F7
F
Piano Solo
Em
C♯7♯9
25
Emaj7
G
Fills (Bridge)
Bm7♭5
E7
Am
B♭m7
E♭7
Am7
D7
Gmaj7
C♯9♯11
H
Head (last 8)
C7
B7♭13
Em
C♯7♯9
F♯7♯9(♭13)
B7♭13
Em
C♯m7♭5
F♯m9
B7♭13
Em
A7
rit.
Freely
C7
B7♭9
Em11

Angel Eyes

(Sonny Criss' solo)

from *Sonny Criss: Saturday Morning*

Words by Earl Brent

Music by Matt Dennis

*Originally performed on Alto Saxophone.

F♯m7♭5 B7♭13 Em C7 Em C♯m7♭5 C7 B7♭13
E
Solo
Em Em
C♯m7♭5 F♯m7♭5 B7♭13
Em C♯m7♭5 C7 B7♭13
F
Em B7♭13 Em
C♯m7♭5 F♯m7♭5 B7♭13
Em C♯m7♭5 C7 B7♭13
G
Em B7♭13 Dm7 G7♭13 Cmaj7 Em7 A7
Dm7 G7♭13 Cmaj7
C♯m7 F♯7 Bmaj7 Fm7 B♭7

H
F♯m7
B7
Em
C♯m7♭5
F♯m7♭5
B7♭13
Em
C♯m7♭5
C7
B7♭13
Em
B7♭13
I
Piano Solo
Em
31
J
Head (last half)
Dm7
G7♭13
Cmaj7
Em7 A7
Dm7
G7♭13
Cmaj7
C♯m7
F♯7
Bmaj7
Fm7
B♭7
F♯m7
B7♭13
K
Em
C7
Em
A13♯11
Em
C♯m7♭5
F♯m7♭5
B7♭13
Em
C7
Em
C♯m7♭5
Slowly, freely
C7
B7♯9(♭13)
N.C.
A13♯11

Anthropology

(Charlie Parker's solo)
from *Charlie Parker: Fragments*
By Charlie Parker and Dizzy Gillespie

*Originally performed on Alto Saxophone.

C7 F7 C7 A7 Dm G7
C Dm G7 Em A7 Dm G7
C7 F C
E
E7 A7
D7 G7
F
C Dm G7 C A7
Dm G7 C7 F7 C A7
G
Dm G7 C Dm G7 Em A7

Dm G7 C7 F C
Dm G7 C Dm G7 Em A7
Dm G7 C7 F Fm C
H
E7 A7
D7 G7
I
C Dm G7 Em A7
Dm G7 C7 F7 F♯dim C7
J
Dm G7 C Dm G7 C

Dm
G7
Gm
C7
F
C7
Dm
G7
C
Dm
G7
C
A7
Dm
G7
C7
F
C
K
E7
A7
D7
G7
L
C
Dm
G7
C
Dm
G7
C
C7
F
F♯dim
C
Dm
G7
M
C
Dm
G7
Trumpet Solo
30
N
32
O
32
P
Piano Solo
32
Q
32
D.S. al Fine
(with repeat)

Bags' Groove

(Chris Potter's solo)

from *Chris Potter: Live performance* (Internet Video)

By Milt Jackson

Tenor Saxophone

C
Em7
A7
Dm7
G7
C
Dm7
G7
D
C
F7
C
F7
C
Em7
A7
Dm7
G7
C
Dm7
G7
E
C
F7
C
F7
C
Em7
A7
Dm7
G7
C

F
Dm7 G7 C
F7 C
F7
C Em7 A7 Dm7
G7 C Dm7 G7
G
C F7 C
F7 C
Em7 A7 Dm7 G7
C Dm7 G7

H
C
F7
8va
3
C
(8va)
F7
(8va)
C
Em7
A7
3
Dm7
G7
C
I
Dm7
G7
C
F7
C
F7
C
Em7
A7
Dm7

G7
C
Dm7
3
G7
J
C
3
F7
C
3
F7
C
Em7
3
A7
5
Dm7
3
G7
3
C
Dm7
G7
K
C
8va
7

F7
C
(8va)
F7
(8va)
C
Em7
A7
Dm7
G7
C
Dm7
G7
L
C
F7
C
F7
C
Em7
A7
Dm7
G7
C
Dm7
G7
M
C
F7
8va
C
(8va)
F7

(8va)
C
Em7
A7
Dm7
(8va)
G7
3
N
C
Dm7
G7
C
(8va)
3
3
F7
C
3
F7
C
Em7
A7
Dm7
G7
3
O
Head
C
Dm7
G7
C
3
F7
C
F7
3
3
C
Em7
A7
Dm7
3
3
1.
2.
G7
C
Dm7
G7
3

Cotton Tail

(Ben Webster's solo)

from *Ben Webster: King of the Tenors*

By Duke Ellington

Tenor Saxophone

D
Sax Solo
C
Am7
D7
G7
C
Am7
D7
G7
C
C7/E
F
F♯dim7
C/G
tr
Dm7
G7
C
Am7
D7
G7
C
3
Am7
D7
G7
C
C7/E
F
F♯dim7
C/G
G7
C
E
E7
A7
D7
G7
F
C
Am7
D7
G7
C
Am7
D7
G7
C
C7/E
F
F♯dim7
C/G
G7
G
Cdim7
Growl
3
3
C
Am7
D7
G7
C

D7 G7 C C7/E F F♯dim7 C/G
G7 C H E7 A7
D7 G7
I C Am7 D7 G7 C Am7
3
D7 G7 C C7/E F F♯dim7 C/G
3
G7 J C Am7 D7 G7 C Am7
D7 G7 C C7/E F F♯dim7 C/G
Dm7 G7 C Am7 D7 G7 C Am7
D7 G7 C C7/E F F♯dim7
C/G G7 C K E7
3

A7
D7
G7
L
C
Am7
D7
G7
C
Am7
D7
G7
C
C7/E
F
F♯dim7
C/G
G7
M
C
Am7
D7
G7
C
Am7
D7
G7
C
C7/E
F
F♯dim7
C/G
Dm7
G7
C
Am7
D7
G7
C
Am7
D7
G7
C
C7/E
F
F♯dim7
C/G
G7
C
N
E7
A7
D7
G7
O
C
Am7
D7
G7

C Am7 D7 G7 C C7/E F F♯dim7
C/G G7
P
C Am7 D7 G7
C Am7 D7 G7 C C7/E F F♯dim7
C/G Dm7 G7 C Am7 D7 G7
C Am7 D7 G7 C C7/E
3
F F♯dim7 C/G G7 C
3
Q
E7
A7
D7 G7
R
Head (last 8 bars)
D7 A7♯5(♭9) D7 G7
C C7/E F F♯dim C/G G9 C6 N.C./C

Bernie's Tune

(Scott Hamilton's solo)

from *Scott Hamilton: East of the Sun*

Music by Bernie Miller

E
Bass Solo
Em
30
F♯m7♭5
B7♭9
F
Sax Solo
Em
C9
F♯m7♭5
B7♭9
Em
F♯m7♭5
B7
G
Em
C9
F♯m7♭5
B7♭9
Em
Dm7
G7
H
C
C♯dim
Dm7
D♯dim
Em7
A7
Dm7
G7
C
Am7
Dm7
G7
C
F♯m7♭5
B7♭9
I
Em
C9
F♯m7♭5
B7♭9
Em
F♯m7♭5
B7♭9
J
Em
C9

F♯m7♭5 B7♭9 Em F♯m7♭5 B7
K
Em C9
F♯m7♭5 B7♭9 Em Dm7 G7
L
C Am7 Dm7 D♯dim Em7 A7 Dm7 G7
C Am7 Dm7 G7 C F♯m7♭5 B7♭9
M
Em C9
F♯m7♭5 B7♭9 Em F♯m7♭5 B7♭9
N
Em C9
sfzp sfzp
F♯m7♭5 B7♭9 Em F♯m7♭5 B7

O
Em
C9
F♯m7♭5
B7♭9
Em
Dm7
G7
P
C
Am7
Dm7
G7
Em7
A7
Dm7
G7
C
Am7
Dm7
G7
C
F♯m7♭5
B7♭9
Q
Em
C9
F♯m7♭5
B7♭9
Em
F♯m7♭5
B7♭9
R
Piano Solo
Em
30
S
Trade 8's (Tenor)
Em
C9
F♯m7♭5
B7♭9
Em
F♯m7♭5
B7

T
(Drums)
Em
7
U
(Sax)
C
Am7
Dm7
G7
Em7
A7
Dm7
G7
C
Am7
Dm7
G7
C
3
F♯m7♭5
B7♭9
V
(Drums)
Em
6
W
Trade 4's
(Sax)
F♯m7♭5
B7♭9
Em
C9
(Drums)
4
X
(Sax)
Em
C9
(Drums)
F♯m7♭5
2
Dm7
G7
Y
(Sax)
C
Am7
Dm7
G7
Em7
A7
Dm7
G7
3
(Drums)
C
Am7
2
F♯m7♭5
B7♭9
Z
(Sax)
Em

(Drums)
C9
F♯m7♭5
3
AA
Head
Em
C9
tr
F♯m7♭5
B7♭9
Em
F♯m7♭5
B7
BB
Em
C9
tr
F♯m7♭5
B7♭9
Em
Dm7
G7
CC
C
Am7
Dm7
G7
Em7
A7
Dm7
G7
C
Am7
Dm7
G7
C
F♯m7♭5
B7♭9
DD
Em
C9
tr
F♯m7♭5
B7♭9
Em
tr
A13♯11

Body and Soul

(Coleman Hawkins' solo)

from *Coleman Hawkins: Body and Soul*

Words by Edward Heyman, Robert Sour and Frank Eyton

Music by John Green

Dm7♭5 G7 Cm7 Fm7 B♭7
E♭ B7 C E F♯m7
G♯m7 Am7 D7 G♯m7 C♯7 F♯m7 B7
E Em7 A7
F♯m7 Fdim7 Em7 A7 6
D7 D♭7 C7 D Fm C7
Fm7 E7 E♭ A♭
Gm7 G♭dim7 Fm7
Dm7♭5 G7 Cm7 E

E Solo
E♭ C7 Fm C7
Fm7 E7 E♭ A♭
Gm7 G♭dim7 Fm7
Dm7♭5 G7 Cm7 Fm7 B♭7
F
E♭ Fm C7
Fm7 B♭7 E♭ A♭
Gm7 G♭dim7 Fm7
Dm7♭5 G7 Cm7 Fm7 B♭7
G
E♭ B7 E F♯m7

G♯m7
Am7
D7
G♯m7
C♯7
F♯m7
B7
E
Em7
A7
F♯m7
Fdim7
Em7
A7
3
D7
D♭7
C7
H
Fm
C7
Fm7
E7
E♭
A♭
Gm7
G♭dim7
Fm7
Cadenza
Rubato
Dm7♭5
G7
Cm7
3
N.C.
E♭

Cherokee

(Indian Love Song)

(Eddie "Lockjaw" Davis' solo)

from *The Best of Johnny Griffin*

Words and Music by Ray Noble

Tenor Saxophone

Very fast (𝅗𝅥 = 168)

Intro 7 — 3

(A) **Head**

C | C7 | Fmaj7 | B♭7♯11 | C | D7

Dm7 | G7 | Dm7 | G7♯5

(B) C | C7 | Fmaj7 | B♭7♯11 | C | D7 | Dm7 | G7 | C

(C) D♯m7 | G♯7 | C♯maj7 | C♯m7 | F♯7 — 3 | B

Bm7 | E7 | Amaj7 | Am7

D
D7
Dm7
G7
C
C7
Fmaj7
B♭7♯11
C
D7
Dm7
G7
C
E
Sax Solo
C7
Fmaj7
B♭7♯11
C
D7
Dm7
G7
Dm7
G7♯5
F
C
C7
Fmaj7
B♭7♯11
C
D7

Dm7
G7
C
G
D♯m7
G♯7
C♯maj7
C♯m7
F♯7
B
Bm7
E7
Amaj7
Am7
D7
Dm7
G7
H
C
C7
Fmaj7
B♭7♯11
C
D7
Dm7
G7
C
I
C7

Fmaj7
B♭7♯11
C
D7
Dm7
G7
Dm7
G7♯5
J
C
C7
Fmaj7
B♭7♯11
C
D7
Dm7
G7
C
K
D♯m7
G♯7
C♯maj7
C♯m7
F♯7
B

Bm7
E7
Amaj7
Am7
D7
Dm7
G7
3
L
C
3
C7
Fmaj7
B♭7♯11
C
D7
Dm7
G7
C
M
C7
Fmaj7
B♭7♯11
C
D7
3
3

Dm7
G7
Dm7
G7♯5
N
C
C7
Fmaj7
B♭7♯11
C
D7
Dm7
G7
C
O
D♯m7
G♯7
C♯maj7
C♯m7
F♯7
B
Bm7
E7
Amaj7
Am7
D7
Dm7
G7

P
C
C7
Fmaj7
B♭7♯11
C
D7
Dm7
G7
C
Q
C7
Fmaj7
B♭7♯11
C
D7
3
Dm7
G7
Dm7
G7♯5
3
R
C
3
C7

Fmaj7
B♭7♯11
C
D7
Dm7
G7
C
S
D♯m7
G♯7
C♯maj7
C♯m7
F♯7
B
Bm7
E7
Amaj7
Am7
D7
Dm7
G7
T
C
C7
Fmaj7
B♭7♯11
C
D7

Dm7
G7
C
Piano Solo
127
Drum Solo
64
Sax Solo
C
C7
Fmaj7
B♭7♯11
C
D7
Dm7
G7
Dm7
G7♯5
C
C7
Fmaj7
B♭7♯11
C
D7
Dm7

Y
G7
C
D♯m7
G♯7
C♯maj7
C♯m7
F♯7
B
Bm7
E7
3
Amaj7
Am7
D7
Dm7
G7
Z
Head (last 16)
C
C7
Fmaj7
B♭7♯11
C
D7
Dm7
G7
Freely
C
3
3
3
3

Donna Lee

(Joe Lovano's solo)
from *Joe Lovano: Bird Songs*
By Charlie Parker

F♯m7
B7♭9
Em7
A7♭9
Dmaj7
Cdim
Dm7
G7♭9
A
Solo
Cm7
F7♭9
B♭maj7
G7
C7
Cm7
F7
B♭maj7
B
Fm7
B♭7
E♭maj7
A♭7
B♭maj7
G7
C7

Cm7
F7
C
B♭maj7
G7
C7
D7
3
Gm7
Am7♭5
D7
3
D
Gm7
D7♭9
Gm7
C♯dim
3
Dm7
G7♭9
Cm7
F7♭9
B♭maj7
3

Cm7
F7
E
B♭maj7
G7
C7
Cm7
F7
B♭maj7
F
Fm7
B♭7
E♭maj7
A♭7
B♭maj7
G7
C7
Cm7

G
F7
B♭maj7
G7
C7
3
D7
Gm7
Am7♭5
H
D7♭9
C♯dim
Dm7
G7♭9
Cm7
F7♭9
rit.
6
Freely
Bmaj7
B♭maj7

Emily

(Frank Morgan's solo)

from *Frank Morgan and the McCoy Tyner Trio: Major Changes*

Music by Johnny Mandel

Words by Johnny Mercer

*Originally performed on Alto Saxophone.

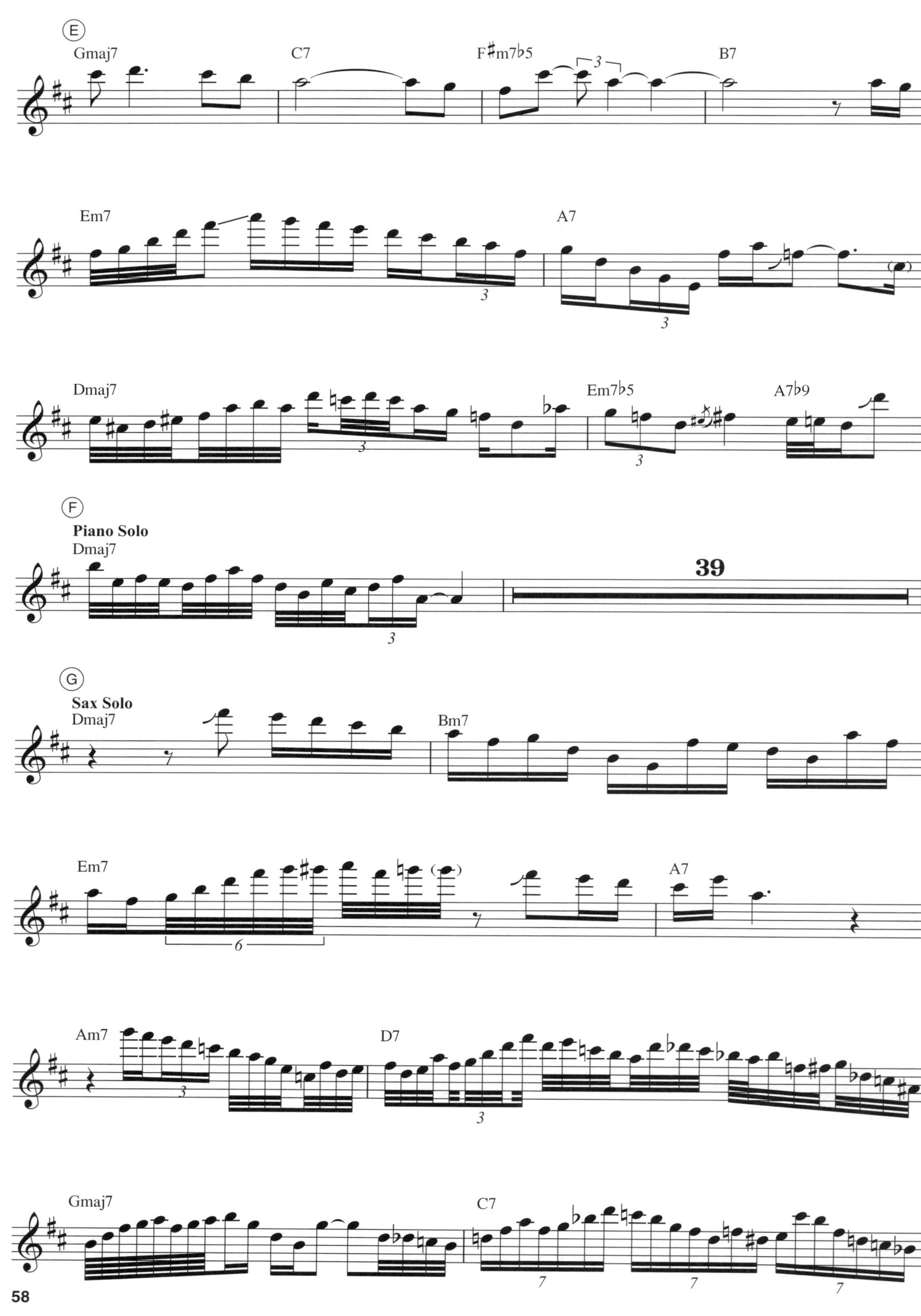
E
Gmaj7
C7
F♯m7♭5
B7
Em7
A7
Dmaj7
Em7♭5
A7♭9
F
Piano Solo
Dmaj7
39
G
Sax Solo
Dmaj7
Bm7
Em7
A7
Am7
D7
Gmaj7
C7

H
Bmaj7
G♯m7
C♯m7
F♯7
Bm7
E7
Em7
A7
I
Dmaj7
Bm7
Em7
A7
Am7
D7
Gmaj7
C♯m7♭5
F♯7♯9
J
Bm
G♯m7♭5
C♯7

F♯m7
B7
Em7
A7
F♯m7♭5
B7
K
Gmaj7
C7
F♯m7♭5
B7
Em7
A7
Dmaj7
Em7♭5
A7♭9
L
Head
Dmaj7
Bm7
Em7
A7
Am7
D7
Gmaj7
C7
M
Bmaj7

G♯m7
C♯m7
F♯7
Bm7
E7
Em7
A7
N
Dmaj7
Bm7
Em7
A7
Am7
D7
Gmaj7
C♯m7♭5 F♯7♯9
O
Bm
G♯m7♭5
C♯7
F♯m7
B7
Em7
A7
F♯m7♭5
B7
P
Gmaj7
C7
F♯m7♭5
B7
Em7
A7
Freely
rit.
Dmaj7

Everything Happens to Me

(Eric Alexander's solo)

from *Eric Alexander: Second Impression*

Words by Johnny Mercer

Music by Hoagy Carmichael

Tenor Saxophone

Fmaj7
D7♭9
Gm7
C7♭9(♭13)
Fmaj7
F♯m7♭5
B7♯9
Emaj7
Am
Am(maj7)
D7sus
D7
D7♯5
G7
D
F♯m7♭5
Fm7
Em7
E♭dim
Dm7
G7
Fm7
B♭7
Em7
A7
C♯dim
Dm7♭5
Em7
E♭dim
Dm7
G7
C
A7♭9
E
Twice as fast
Sax Solo
Dm7
G7♭9
Em7
E♭dim
Dm7
G7
B♭7
A7
C♯dim

Dm7♭5
Em7
E♭dim
Dm7
G7
Em7
A7♭9
F
Dm7
G7♭9
Em7
E♭dim
Dm7
G7
B♭7
A7
C♯dim
Dm7♭5
Em7
E♭dim
Dm7
G7
C
G
Gm7
C7
Fmaj7
D7
Gm7
C7
Fmaj7

F♯m7♭5
B7♭13
Emaj7
Am
D7sus
D7
H
A♭7
G7
F♯m7♭5
Fm7
Em7
E♭dim
Dm7
G7
B♭7
A7
C♯dim
Dm7♭5
Em7
E♭dim
Dm7
G7
C
A7
I
Piano Solo
30
Am7
A♭7
J
Head (2nd half)
Gm7
C7♯9
Fmaj7

D7♭9
Gm7
C7♭9
Fmaj7
F♯m7♭5
B7♭13
5
Emaj7
Am
Am(maj7)
D7sus
D7
K
Tempo I
A♭7
G7
F♯m7♭5
Fm
Em7
E♭dim
Dm7
G7
B♭7sus
B♭7
A7sus
A7
Slowly, freely
C♯dim
Dm7♭5
Em7
E♭dim
Dm7
rit.
G13♭9
C13
B13♭9
B♭13
A13♯9
A♭13
D♭maj7/G
Cmaj13♯11
3
3

A Foggy Day

(In London Town)

(Lester Young's solo)

from *Lester Young: Intégrale Jazz Vol. 5*

Music and Lyrics by George Gershwin and Ira Gershwin

C Sax Solo
F6/9
D7♯5(♭9)
G9
C7♯5(♭9)
F6/9
A♭9
G9
C7♯5(♯9)
Cm7/F
Cm9
F13
B♭maj13
E♭9
Am7
D7sus
D7
G9
C7♭9
D
F6/9
D7♯5(♭9)
G9
C7♯5(♭9)
F6/9
A♭9
G9
C7♯5(♭9)
Cm7/F
Cm9
F13
B♭maj13
E♭9
Fmaj7
Gm7
Fmaj7
Gm7
Fmaj7
D7♯5(♭9)
Gm7
C13♭9
F6
N.C./C
C7♯5(♯9)
E
F6/9
D7♯5(♭9)

G9
C7♯5(♭9)
F6/9
Growl
A♭9
G9
C7♯5(♯9)
Cm7/F
Cm9
F13
B♭maj13
E♭9
Am7
D7sus
D7
F
G9
C7♭9
F6/9
D7♯5(♭9)
G9
C7♯5(♭9)
F6/9
A♭9
G9
C7♯5(♭9)
Cm7/F
Cm9
F13
B♭maj13
E♭9
Fmaj7
Gm7
Fmaj7
Gm7
Fmaj7
D7♯5(♭9)
Gm7
C13♭9
F6
N.C./C
C7♯5(♯9)
G
Trumpet Solo
F6/9
33
H
34
I
Piano Solo
34
J
Bass Solo
34

K
Sax Solo
F6/9 D7♯5(♭9) G9 C7♯5(♭9)
F6/9 A♭9 G9 C7♯5(♯9)
Cm7/F Cm9 F13 B♭maj13
E♭9 Am7 D7sus D7
G9 C7♭9
L
F6/9 D7♯5(♭9)
G9 C7♯5(♭9) F6/9 A♭9
Lay back
G9 C7♯5(♭9) Cm7/F Cm9 F13
8va
B♭maj13 E♭9 Fmaj7 Gm7 Fmaj7 Gm7
Fmaj7 D7♯5(♭9) Gm7 C13♭9 F6 N.C./C C7♯5(♯9)

M
Trading 4's
F6/9
3
F6/9
A♭9
G9
C7♯5(♯9)
Cm7/F
3
Am7
D7sus
D7
G9
C7♭9
N
F6/9
3
F6/9
A♭9
G9
C7♯5(♭9)
Cm7/F
Cm9
F13
B♭maj13
E♭9
Fmaj7
Gm7
O
Tag (Latin feel)
Fmaj7
Gm7
Fmaj7
D7♯5(♭9)
Gm7
C13♭9
F6/9
Gm7
Gm7/C
F6/9
Gm7
Gm7/C
F6/9
Gm7
Gm7/C
F

Flying Home

(Illinois Jacquet's solo)

from *Illinois Jacquet: Flying Home – The Best of the Verve Years*

Music by Benny Goodman and Lionel Hampton

Tenor Saxophone

D
Sax Solo
B♭ B♭7/D E♭ Edim B♭/F Gm7 C7 F7
B♭ B♭/A♭ E♭/G Edim B♭/F G7 C7 F7
E
B♭ B♭7/D E♭ Edim B♭/F Gm7 C7 F7
B♭ B♭7/D E♭ Edim B♭/F F7
3
F
B♭ B♭7 E♭
C7 F7
G
B♭ B♭7/D E♭ Edim B♭/F Gm7
C7 F7 B♭ B♭7/D E♭ Edim
3

H
Bb/F
Gm7
C7
F7
Bb
Bb7/D
Eb
Edim
Bb/F
Gm7
C7
F7
Bb
Bb/Ab
Eb/G
Edim
I
Bb/F
G7
C7
F7
Bb
Bb7/D
Eb
Edim
Bb/F
Gm7
C7
F7
Bb
Bb7/D
Eb
Edim
J
Bb/F
F7
Bb
Bb7
Eb
C7
K
F7b9
Bb
Bb7/D
Eb
Edim
Bb/F
Gm7
C7
F7
Bb
Bb7/D
Eb
Edim
(Solo break)
Bb/F
Fdim
F7sus
Bb

L
Eb
Eb/G
Ab
Adim
Eb/Bb
Cm7
Fm7
Bb7sus
Eb
Eb/G
Ab
Adim
1.
Eb/Bb
Cm7
Fm7
Bb7sus
2.
Eb/Bb
Cm7
Fm7
Bb7sus
M
Eb7
Ab7
F7
unison
N
Eb
Eb/Db
Ab/C
Adim
Eb/Bb
Cm7
Fm7
Bb7sus
Eb
Eb7/G
Ab
Adim
unison
E9#11
Eb6/9

Footprints

(Wayne Shorter's solo)
from *Wayne Shorter: Adam's Apple*
By Wayne Shorter

*Originally performed on Alto Saxophone.

E13
A9
F♯m7♭5
To Coda
B7
Dm7
C
Sax Solo
Dm7
Gm7
Dm7
E13
A9
F♯m7♭5
B7
Dm7
D
Dm7

Gm7
Dm7
tr
2
E13
A9
F♯m7♭5
B7
Dm7
E
Dm7
Gm7
Dm7
E13
A9

F♯m7♭5
B7
Dm7
tr
tr
F
Dm7
Gm7
Dm7
E13
A9
3
F♯m7♭5
B7
Dm7
G
Piano Solo
71
(3 Choruses)
H
Bass Solo
48
(2 Choruses)
D.S. al Coda
CODA
Dm7

Frenesi

(Benny Carter's solo)

from *Cosmopolite: The Oscar Peterson Verve Sessions*

Words and Music by Alberto Dominguez

*Originally performed on Alto Saxophone.

N.C.
C13 C♯13 D13
G
Em7
Am7
D7
G
N.C.
E
Sax Solo
Am7
D7
Am7
D7
G
C
G
Bm7
E7
F
Am7
D7
Am7
D7
G
C
G
C♯m7
F♯7
G
B
C♯m7
F♯7
B
C♯m7
F♯7
B
Em7
H
Am7
D7
Am7
D7

Am7 D7 G C
G Bm7 E7 I Am7 D7
Am7 D7 G
C G Bm7 E7 J Am7
D7 Am7 D7
G C G
C♯m7 F♯7 K B C♯m7 F♯7
B C♯m7 F♯7 B
Em7 Am7 D7
L Am7 D7 Am7

D7
G
C
G
Bm7
E7
M
Am7
D7
Am7
D7
G
C
3
G
Bm7
E7
N
Am7
D7
Am7
D7
G
C
G
C♯m7
F♯7
O
B
C♯m7
F♯7
B
C♯m7
F♯7
B
Em7
Am7
D7
P
Am7
D7
Am7
D7
G
C
G
Bm7
E7

Q
Piano Solo
Am7
D7
31
R
31
S
Sax Solo
Am7
D7
Am7
D7
G
C
G
Bm7
E7
T
Am7
D7
Am7
D7
G
C
G
C♯m7
F♯7
U
B
C♯m7
F♯7
B
C♯m7
F♯7
B
Em7
Am7
D7
V
Am7
D7
Am7
D7
G
C
G
Bm7
E7
W
Am7

D7
Am7
D7
G
Bdim
C
C♯dim
G
Bm7
E7
X
Am7
D7
Am7
D7
G
Bdim
C
C♯dim
G
C♯m7
F♯7
Y
B
C♯m7
F♯7
B
Em7
Am7
D7
Z
Head (Last 8)
C13
C♯13
D13
N.C.
C13
C♯13
D13
N.C.
G
Bdim
C
C♯dim
Am7
D7
G

Georgia on My Mind

(Gene Ammon's solo)

from *Gene Ammons & Dodo Marmarosa: Jug & Dodo*

Words by Stuart Gorrell

Music by Hoagy Carmichael

Tenor Saxophone

C
Cm7
Cm7/F F7♭9
B♭maj7
Am7
D7♭9
Gm
Gm7
C7
E♭m7/D♭ E♭m6/D♭
Dm7
G9
Cm9
F13
B♭maj7
E♭maj9
B♭maj7
D Sax Solo
B♭maj7
Double-time feel
Am7
D7♭9
Gm
Gm7
C9
C♯dim7
Dm7
G7
Cm7
F7
Dm7
G7♭9
Cm7
F7♭9
B♭maj7
Am7
D7♭9
Gm
Gm7
C9
C♯dim7
Dm7
G7

Cm7
F7
B♭maj7
E♭maj7
B♭maj7
D7♭9
E
Gm7
E♭9
Gm7
E♭9
Gm7
E♭9
Gm7
C9
Gm7
C♯dim7
Dm7
C♯m9
Cm9
F13
F
B♭maj7
Am7
D7♭9
Gm
Gm7

C9
C♯dim7
Dm7
G7
Cm7
F7
B♭maj7
E♭6/9
Lay back
B♭maj7
G Piano Solo
Gm
6
H Head (last section)
B♭maj7
Am7
D7♭9
Gm
Gm7
C7
E♭m7/D♭
E♭m6/D♭
Dm7
G9
Cm9
F13
Freely
N.C.
accel.
rit.
Freely
B♭maj7

Giant Steps

(John Coltrane's solo)

from *John Coltrane: Giant Steps*

By John Coltrane

Tenor Saxophone

Gm7
C7
F
Bm7
E7
A
E♭m7
A♭7
D♭
D
E
* Fingered as D, overtone sounds as A

A Ebm7 Ab7 Db Gm7 C7
RUSH
F Ebm7 Ab7
F
Db E7 A C7
F Bm7 E7 A C7 F Ab7
Db Gm7 C7 F Bm7 E7
A Ebm7 Ab7 Db
3
Gm7 C7 F Ebm7 Ab7
G
Db E7 A C7 F B7 E7
A C7 F Ab7 Db Gm7 C7
F Bm7 E7 A
Ebm7 Ab7 Db Gm7 C7
3
F Ebm7 Ab7
H
Db E7 A C7

F
Bm7
E7
A
C7
F
Ab7
Db
Gm7
C7
F
Bm7
E7
A
Ebm7
Ab7
Db
Gm7
C7
F
Ebm7
Ab7
I
Db
E7
A
C7
F
Bm7
E7
A
C7
F
Ab7
Db
Gm7
C7
F
Bm7
E7
A
Ebm7
Ab7
Db
Gm7
C7
F
Ebm7
Ab7
J
Db
E7
A
C7
F
Bm7
E7
A
C7
F
Ab7
Db
Gm7
C7
F
Bm7
E7
A
Ebm7
Ab7

D♭ Gm7 C7 F E♭m7 A♭7
K
D♭ E7 A C7 F Bm7 E7
A C7 F A♭7 D♭ Gm7 C7
F Bm7 E7 A E♭m7 A♭7
D♭ Gm7 C7 F E♭m7 A♭7
L
D♭ E7 A C7 F
Bm7 E7 A C7 F A♭7
D♭ RUSH Gm7 C7 F Bm7 E7
A E♭m7 A♭7 D♭ Gm7 C7
F E♭7 A♭7
M
D♭ E7 A C7
F Bm7 E7 A C7 F A♭7

D♭ Gm7 C7 F
Bm7 E7 A E♭m7 A♭7
D♭ Gm7 C7 F E♭m7 A♭7
N D♭ E7 A C7 F 13 O 16
P 16 Q 16 R D♭ E7 A C7
F Bm7 E7 A C7
F A♭7 D♭ Gm7 C7
F Bm7 E7 A E♭m7 A♭7
D♭ Gm7 C7 F E♭m7 A♭7
S D♭ E7 A C7 F Bm7 E7
A C7 F A♭7 D♭ Gm7 C7

F
Bm7
E7
A
E♭m7
A♭7
D♭
Gm7
C7
F
E♭m7
A♭7
T
Head
D♭
E7
A
C7
F
Bm7
E7
A
C7
F
A♭7
D♭
Gm7
C7
F
Bm7
E7
A
E♭m7
A♭7
D♭
Gm7
C7
F
E♭m7
A♭7
U
D♭
E7
A
C7
F
Bm7
E7
A
C7
F
A♭7
D♭
Gm7
C7
F
Bm7
E7
A
E♭m7
A♭7
D♭
Gm7
C7
F (Hold on F)

I Can't Give You Anything but Love

(James Carter's solo)

from *Amazing Keystone Big Band au Festival Django Reinhardt 2015* (Internet Video)

Words and Music by Jimmy McHugh and Dorothy Fields

A7
(8va)
D
B7
Em7
A7
E
Guitar Solo
D
15
F
Trumpet Solo
16
G
Sax Solo
D
G7
F♯m7
B7
Em7
A7
D
G7
F♯m7
B7
Em7
A7
H
Am7
D7
G
E7
8va
A7sus
I
D
G7
F♯m7
B7
Em7
A7

Am7
D7
G
J
G♯dim
D/A
B7
8va
Em7
A7
D
B7
Em7
A7
(8va)
K
D
G7
F♯m7
B7
Em7
A7
(8va)
D
G7
F♯m7
B7
Em7
A7
(8va)
L
Am7
D7
G
E7

A7sus
M
D
G7
F♯m7
B7
Em7
A7
Am7
D7
G
N
G♯dim
D/A
B7
8va
Em7
(8va)
A7
D
B7
Em7
A7
O
Head
D
G7
F♯m7
B7
Em7
A7
D
G7
F♯m7
B7
Em7
A7

P
Am7
D7
G
E7
A7sus
15ma
Q
D
G7
F♯m7
B7
Em7
A7
Am7
D7
G
R
G♯dim
D/A
B7
Outro
Em7
A7
F♯m7♭5
B7
Em7
A13sus
8va
D
G7
A7♯5
D
D13
Slowly, freely
(8va)

Ginger Bread Boy

(Jimmy Heath's solo)

from *Jimmy Heath Quintet: On the Trail*

By Jimmy Heath

Tenor Saxophone

Medium Bop (♩ = 212)

Ⓐ **Head**

N.C./C /G /D /G /C C7♯9

N.C./F /G♭ /F /G /C C7♯9

C7♯5(♯9) A7♯5(♭9) D7♭5(♭9) G7♯5(♯9)

C7♯9

1.

2.

Ⓑ **Guitar Solo**

12 12 12 12 12

Ⓒ **Sax Solo**

C7 F7

C7 3 A7 Dm7

G13 C G7

D
C7
F7
C7
A7
Dm7
G13
C
G7
E
C7
F7
C7
A7
Dm7
G13
C
G7
F
C7
F7
C7
A7

Dm7
G13
C
G7
G
C7
F7
C7
A7
Dm7
G13
C
G7
H
C7
F7
C7
A7
Dm7
G13
C
G7
3
I
C7

F7
C7
A7
Dm7
G13
C
G7
J
C7
Piano Solo
8
12
12
12
12
12
12
11
K Head
N.C./C
/G
/D
/G
/C
C7♯9
N.C./F
/G♭
/F
/G
/C
C7♯9
C7♯5(♯9)
A7♯5(♭9)
D7♭5(♭9)
G7♯5(♯9)
1.
C7♯9
2.
Vamp ad lib. and Fade
C7♯9

Groovin' High

(Art Pepper's solo)

from *Art Pepper + Eleven*

By John "Dizzy" Gillespie

*Tenor Saxophone

*Originally performed on Alto Saxophone.

To Coda
Gm7
C7
Gm7
Gm7♭5
E
D♭maj7
G♭maj7
C♭maj7
F♭maj7
Fmaj7
C7sus
F
Sax Soli
F
Bm7
E9sus
E9
F
Am7
D9sus
D9
G
G
Gm7
C13sus
C7♭9(♭13)
Am7
A♭m7
Gm7
H
Trumpet Solo
C7♭9
F
13
I
Sax Solo
F
Gm7
C7
F
Bm7
E7
F

Am7
D7
J
G
Gm7
C7
Am7
G♯m7
Gm7
C7
K
F
Bm7
E7
F
Am7
D7
L
G
Gm7
C7
Gm7
C7
F
Gm7
C7
M
F
Bm7
E7
F
Am7
D7
N
G
Gm7

C7
Am7
G♯m7
Gm7
C7
O
F
Bm7
E7
F
Am7
D7
P
G
Gm7
C7
Gm7
C7
Q
F
Gm7
C7
F
3
E7
F
Am7
D7
R
G
Gm7
C7
3
C7
D.S. al Coda
CODA
D♭maj7
G♭maj7
C13♯11
F7♯9(♭13)
B♭13♯11
E♭7♯9(♭13)
A♭13♯11
D♭7♯9(♭13)
G♭13♯11
Fmaj13

Hot House

(Ernie Watts' solo)

from *Ernie Watts: To the Point*

By Tadd Dameron

8va
(8va)

8va
8va
Fast Swing (♩ = 296)
Intro

A
Head
Am7♭5
D7♯5
Gm7♭5
C7♯5
Em7♭5
A7♯5
Dmaj7
3
B
Am♭5
D7♯5
Gm7♭5
C7♯5
Em7♭5
A7♯5
Dmaj7
3
3
C
Dm7
G7
3
Cmaj7
B♭7
A7

D
Am7b5
D7#5
Gm7b5
C7#5
Em7b5
A7#5
Dmaj7
Fine
E Sax Solo
Am7b5
D7#5
Gm7b5
C7#5
Em7b5
A7#5
Dmaj7
F
Amb5
D7#5
Gm7b5
C7#5
Em7b5
A7#5
Dmaj7
G
Dm7
G7
Cmaj7
Bb7
A7
H
Am7b5
D7#5
Gm7b5
C7#5
Em7b5
A7#5
Dmaj7

I
Am7♭5
D7♯5
Gm7♭5
C7♯5
Em7♭5
3
A7♯5
Dmaj7
8va
3
J
Am♭5
(8va)
D7♯5
Gm7♭5
C7♯5
Em7♭5
A7♯5
Dmaj7
K
Dm7
G7
Cmaj7
B♭7
A7
L
Am7♭5
D7♯5
Gm7♭5
3
C7♯5
Em7♭5
3
A7♯5
Dmaj7
M
Am7♭5
D7♯5
Gm7♭5
C7♯5
Em7♭5
A7♯5

N
Dmaj7
Am♭5
D7♯5
Gm7♭5
C7♯5
Em7♭5
A7♯5
O
Dmaj7
Dm7
G7
Cmaj7
B♭7
P
A7
Am7♭5
D7♯5
Gm7♭5
C7♯5
Em7♭5
A7♯5
Q
Dmaj7
Am7♭5
D7♯5
Gm7♭5
C7♯5
Em7♭5
A7♯5
Dmaj7
R
Am♭5
D7♯5
Gm7♭5
C7♯5

Em7♭5
A7♯5
Dmaj7
8va
S
Dm7
(8va)
G7
Cmaj7
B♭7
A7
T
Am7♭5
D7♯5
Gm7♭5
C7♯5
Em7♭5
A7♯5
Dmaj7
U
Am7♭5
D7♯5
Gm7♭5
C7♯5
Em7♭5
A7♯5
Dmaj7
V
Am♭5
D7♯5
Gm7♭5
C7♯5
Em7♭5
A7♯5
Dmaj7
W
Dm7
G7
Cmaj7

B♭7
A7
X
Am7♭5
D7♯5
Gm7♭5
C7♯5
Em7♭5
A7♯5
Dmaj7
Y
Am7♭5
D7♯5
Gm7♭5
C7♯5
Em7♭5
A7♯5
Dmaj7
Z
8va
Am♭5
D7♯5
Gm7♭5
C7♯5
Em7♭5
A7♯5
Dmaj7
AA
Dm7
G7
Cmaj7
B♭7

BB
A7
Am7♭5
D7♯5
Gm7♭5
C7♯5
Em7♭5
A7♯5
CC
Dmaj7
Piano Solo
96
DD
Trade 8's
Am7♭5
D7♯5
Gm7♭5
C7♯5
Em7♭5
A7♯5
Dmaj7
Drums
8
Piano
8
Drums
8
Am7♭5
8va
D7♯5
Gm7♭5
C7♯5
Em7♭5
A7♯5
Dmaj7
D.S. al Fine
Drums
8
Piano
8
Drums
7

I Hadn't Anyone Till You

(Houston Person's solo)
from *Houston Person: Blue Velvet*
Words and Music by Ray Noble

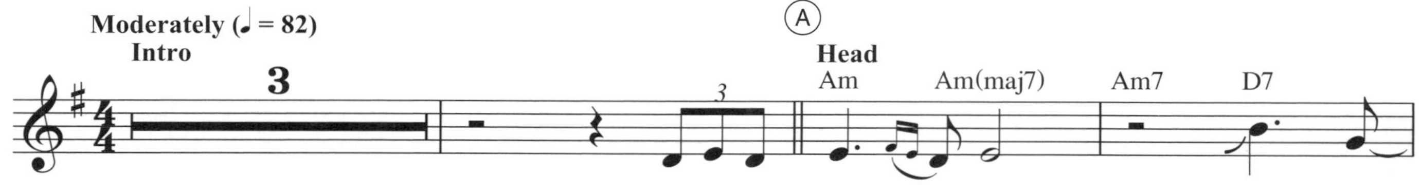

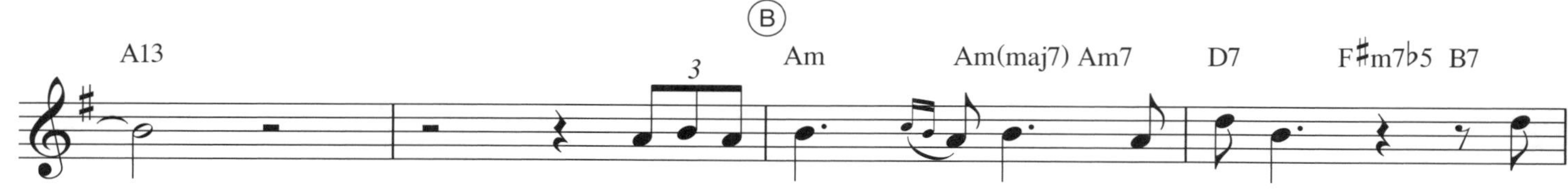

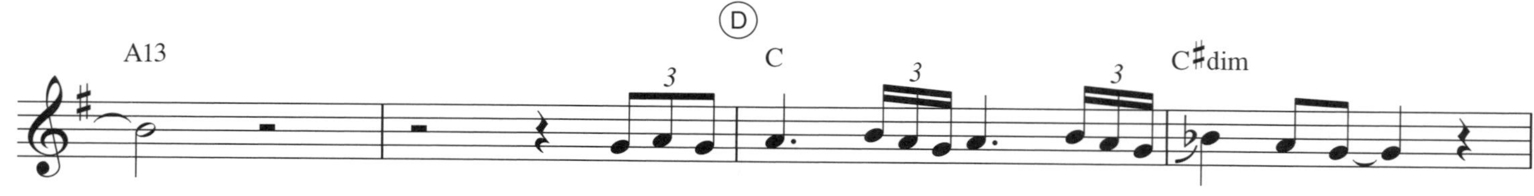

G7
F♯7
Bm7♭5
E7♯9(♭13)
Am7
Bm7
E7♭9
Am7
C♯dim
D7♭9
G
Bm7
E7
E
Piano Solo
16
F
Sax Solo
Am7
D7
G6
Am7
A♯dim
G/B
C♯m7♭5
F♯7
Bm7
E7
A13
G
C
C♯dim
G7
F♯7
Bm7♭5
E7♯9(♭13)
Am7
Bm7
E7♭9
Am7
D7♭9
G
Bm7
E7
H
Am7
D7
G6
Am7
A♯dim
G/B
C♯m7♭5
F♯7

Bm7
E7
A13
5
6
I
Am
D7
F♯m7♭5
B7
Em7
Em/D
3
C♯m7♭5
F♯7♭9
Bmaj7
G♯m7
C♯13
F♯7
B13
E9
Am7
D7
G♯dim
J
Head (2nd half)
G6
A♯dim
G/B
C♯m7♭5
K
C
C♯dim
G7
Bm7♭5
E7♯9(♭13)
E7♭9
D7♭9
Cm7
F9
B♭m9
E♭9
Am9
D9
A♭7
Gmaj9

I Love Paris

(Buddy Collette's solo)
from *Buddy Collette: Jazz Loves Paris*
Words and Music by Cole Porter

Tenor Saxophone

D
E
Sax Solo
Em7♭5
A7♭9
F
A7
Dm7
G
D
Bm7
E7
Em7
A7

H
Gmaj7
Em7
F♯m7
B7♭9
Em7
A7♭9
Dm
Em7♭5
A7
I
Trombone Solo
Dm
15
J
Guitar Solo
D
Em7
A7
9
K
Head (last eight)
Gmaj7
G/F♯
Em7
Dmaj9
F♯m7♭5/B
B7♭9
Em7
D♯dim
Em7 A7sus
A7
D
Tresillo
L
Outro
Dm7
4
E♭ locrian
D5
Dm9

I Remember Clifford

(Bud Shank's solo)

from *By Request: Bud Shank Meets the Rhythm Section*

By Benny Golson

*Originally performed on Alto Saxophone.

Dm Dm/C Bm7♭5 E7♭9
Am7 D7 Gm7 C7 Fmaj7 A7♭13 B♭maj7 Bdim
D
C7 C♯dim Dm Dm/C
Bm7♭5 E7♭9 Am7♭5 D7♭9 Gm7 C7♭9(♭13)
E
Sax Solo
Fmaj7 C13♭9 Fmaj7 A7♭13
B♭maj7 Bdim C7 C♯dim
Dm Dm/C Bm7♭5 E7
Am Am/G F♯m7♭5 B7
F
Gm7 C7♭9 Fmaj7 A7♭13
B♭maj7 Bdim C7 C♯dim

Dm
Dm/C
Bm7b5
E7b9
Am7b5
D7b9
Gm7
C7b13
Am7
Bbmaj7
Bm7b5
G
E7b9
Am7
D7
Gm7
C7b13
Fmaj7
Em7b5
A7b9
Dm
Dm/C
Bm7b5
E7b9
Am7 D7b9
Gm7C7
H
Fmaj7
A7b13
Bbmaj7
Bdim
C7
C#dim
Dm
Dm/C
Bm7b5
E7b9
Am7b5
D7b9
Gm7
C7b13
Fmaj7
C13b9

I
Bass Solo
Fmaj7
tr
14
Am7
B♭maj7
5
6
J
Head (2nd half)
Bm7♭5
E7♭9
Am7
D7♭9
Gm7
C7♯5
3
Fmaj7
3
Em7♭5
A7♯11
A7
3
Dm
Dm/C
6
Bm7♭5
E7♭9
Am7
D7
6
Gm7
C7
3
K
Fmaj7
A7♭13
B♭maj7
Bdim
C7
C♯dim
Dm
Dm/C
Slowly, freely
Bm7♭5
E7♭9
Am7♭5
D7♭9
Gm7
C7♭9(♭13)
F
rit.
L
Outro
B♭maj7
A7♭13
C7♭9
3
A7♭9
Dm7
Cm9
B♭m9
A♭m9
Gm9
C13sus
C7♭9
F

I Remember You

(Spike Robinson's solo)

from *Spike Robinson: A Real Corker*

Words by Johnny Mercer

Music by Victor Schertzinger

Gmaj7
C♯m7♭5
Cm
Bm7
Edim
Am7
D7
E
Sax Solo
G
Gmaj7
C♯m7
F♯7
Gmaj7
Dm7
G7
Cmaj7
Cm7
F7
F
Bm7
E7
Am7
D7
Gmaj7
C♯m7
F♯7
Gmaj7
Dm7
G7
Cmaj7
Cm7
F7
G
Gmaj7
Dm7
G7
Cmaj7
F♯m7
B7
Emaj7
F♯m7
B7
Emaj7
Em7
A7
H
Am7
D7
Gmaj7
C♯m7
F♯7
Gmaj7
Dm7
G7
C
Cm7
F7

Gmaj7 C♯m7♭5 Cm Bm7 Edim Am7 D7
I
G E7 Am7 D7 Gmaj7 C♯m7 F♯7
Gmaj7 Dm7 G7 Cmaj7 Cm7 F7
J
Bm7 E7 Am7 D7 Gmaj7 C♯m7 F♯7
Gmaj7 Dm7 G7 Cmaj7 Cm7 F7
K
Gmaj7 Dm7 G7 Cmaj7 F♯m7 B7
Emaj7 F♯m7 B7 Emaj7 Em7 A7
L
Am7 D7 Gmaj7 C♯m7 F♯7
Gmaj7 Dm7 G7 C Cm7 F7

Gmaj7
C♯m7♭5
Cm
Bm7
Edim
Am7
D7
M
Guitar Solo
G
E7
Am7
D7
Gmaj7
35
N
36
O
Bass Solo
36
P
36
Q
Trade 8's
Gmaj7
C♯m7
F♯7
Gmaj7
Dm7
G7
3
Cmaj7
Cm7
F7
Bm7
E7
Am7
D7
R
Drums
Gmaj7
7
S
Guitar
8
T
Drums
12
U
Gmaj7
3
C♯m7
F♯7
Gmaj7
Dm7
G7
Cmaj7
Cm7
F7
Bm7
E7
Am7
D7
V
Drums
Gmaj7
7
W
Guitar
8

X
Y
Head
Drums
11
Gmaj7
C#m7
F#7
Gmaj7
Dm7
G7
Cmaj7
Cm7
F7
Bm7
E7
Am7
D7
Z
Gmaj7
C#m7
F#7
Gmaj7
Dm7
G7
Cmaj7
Cm7
F7
Gmaj7
Dm7
G7
AA
Cmaj7
F#m7
B7
Emaj7
F#m7
B7
Emaj7
Em7
A7
Am7
D7
BB
Gmaj7
C#m7
F#7
Gmaj7
Dm7
G7
C
F7
G
C#m7♭5
Cm
Bm
E7
Am7
D7
Tag
Dm
C#7
Cm7
F7
Bm
E7
Am7
D7
G

Line for Lyons

(Gerry Mulligan's solo)

from *Gerry Mulligan with Chet Baker and Friends*

By Gerry Mulligan

*Tenor Saxophone

*Originally performed on Baritone Saxophone.

C♯m7 F♯7 Bm7♭5 E7 A F♯7♭9 Bm7 E7
A F♯7♭9 Bm7 E7 Amaj7 Dm7 G7
C♯m7 F♯7 Bm7 E7♭9 A F♯7♭9 3 Bm7 E7♭9
E
(Background w/tpt.)
A6 Dmaj7 G♯7♭9
C♯m(maj7) C♯m7 F♯7sus♭9 F♯7♭9 Bm(maj7) Bm7 E7sus E7
F
Amaj7 B♭dim7 Bm7 E7 A Dm7 G7
C♯m7 F7 Bm7 E7 Amaj7 F♯7♭9 Bm7 E7♯9
G
Amaj7 B♭dim7 Bm7 E7 A Dm7 G7

C♯m7 F♯7 Bm7 E7 A F♯m7 Bm7 E7
Amaj7 F♯7♯11 Bm7 E7 A Dm7 G7
C♯m7 F♯7♭9 Bm7 E7 Amaj7 F♯7♭9 Bm7 E7
H
Amaj7 A7♯11 Dmaj7♭5 G♯7♭9
C♯m(maj7) C♯m7 F♯7♭9 Bm(maj7) Bm7 E7 Amaj9 F♯7♯5(♭9)
I Head
Bm E7 A A7♭9 Dm7 G7 C♯m7 F♯7
Bm7 E7 Amaj7 F♯7♭9 Bm7 E7♭9 A B♭dim7
Bm7 E7 Amaj7 B♭dim7 Bm7 E7sus E7sus♭9 Amaj7

I'm Old Fashioned

(Ravi Coltrane's solo)

from *Glenn Zaleski: My Ideal*

Lyrics by Johnny Mercer

Music by Jerome Kern

Cm11
Dbmaj13#11
5
5
D
Eb6/9
Dbmaj7#5
G7add4
Eb6/9
Abmaj13#11
Bbmaj9
Abmaj13#11
G7sus
Bbm7b5
Eb7
Am7
D7b9#11
Gm
Dbmaj13
3
E
F
G
Moderately fast, steadily (♩ = 132)
Piano Solo
12
36
35
H
Sax Solo
Eb6/9

I
A♭maj13♯5
E♭6/9
G♭maj7♭5
Dm11
G13♭9
J
F13sus
D/F
C/F
A/G
G/F
A/B
G♯m9
E/D
Dm11
K
Cm11
D♭maj13♯11
E♭6/9

D♭maj7♯5
G7add4
E♭6/9
A♭maj13♯11
B♭maj9
A♭maj13♯11
G7sus
B♭m7♭5
E♭7
Am7
D7♭9♯11
Gm
D♭maj13
E♭6/9
L
E♭6/9
M
A♭maj13♯5

E♭6/9
G♭maj7♭5
Dm11
G13♭9
N
F13sus
3
D/F
C/F
A/G
G/F
A/B
G♯m9
E/D
Dm11
Cm11
D♭maj13♯11
O
Head (last 12)
E♭6/9
D♭maj7♯5
G7add4
E♭6/9
A♭maj13♯11
B♭maj9
A♭maj13♯11
G7sus
B♭m7♭5
E♭7
Am7
D7♭9♯11
Gm
D♭maj13

Outro (fills)

Idaho

(Al Cohn's solo)

from *Al Cohn: Cohn on the Saxophone*

Words and Music by Jesse Stone

Am7
D7
Bm7
E7♭9
Am7
D7
Gmaj7
Bm7
E7♭9
Am7
Am7/D
D7
Gmaj7
G
Cm7
F7
B♭maj7
Bm7
E7♭9
A7
D7
Gmaj7
Bm7
E7♭9
Am7
Am7/D
D7
Gmaj7
E7♭9
Am7
D7
H
Gmaj7

Bm7
E7♭9
Am7
D7
Bm7
E7♭9
Am7
D7
Gmaj7
3
Bm7
E7♭9
Am7
Am7/D
D7
Gmaj7
I
Cm7
F7
3
B♭maj7
Bm7
E7♭9
A7
D7
3
Gmaj7
Bm7
E7♭9
Am7
Am7/D
D7
Gmaj7
E7♭9
Am7
D7
J
Trading 4's
Gmaj7
Trombone:
3
Drums:
4
Sax:
Gmaj7

Drums:
Trombone:
Bm7
E7♭9
Am7
3
4
Drums:
Sax:
4
Gmaj7
3
Drums:
Bm7
E7♭9
Am7
2
Piano:
K Head
G
G+
G6
G7
D7/A
C/D
D7
G
G
G+
G6
G7
D7/A
C/D
D7
G
Drums:
L Sax:
8
G
G+
G6
G7
D7/A
C/D
D7
Am7
A♯dim7
Bm7
E7
Am7
D7
G

Inner Urge

(Joe Henderson's solo)

from *Joe Henderson: Inner Urge*

By Joe Henderson

Tenor Saxophone

Moderately fast (♩ = 212)

A

Head

G♯m7♭5

Gmaj7♯11

B

Fmaj7♯11

Emaj7♯11 Fmaj7♯11

E♭sus Esus4 B♭sus2/A E♭maj7♯11

3

D/E♭

C

G♭maj7♭5

E♭maj9

3

Emaj9

D♭maj9

Dmaj13♯11

3

Bmaj9

1. Gm(maj7)

3

Amaj9

2. C13♯11

3

Amaj9

D
Bass Solo
72
E
Sax Solo
G♯ locrian
Gmaj7♭5
F
Fmaj7♭5
E♭maj7♭5
G
F♯maj7
E♭maj7
Emaj7
D♭maj7
Dmaj7
Bmaj7
C13♯11
Amaj7
H
G♯ locrian
Gmaj7♭5
I
Fmaj7♭5

E♭maj7♭5
J
F♯maj7
E♭maj7
Emaj7
D♭maj7
Dmaj7
Bmaj7
C13♯11
Amaj7
K
G♯locrian
Gmaj7♭5
L
Fmaj7♭5
E♭maj7♭5
M
F♯maj7
E♭maj7
Emaj7

D♭maj7
Dmaj7
Bmaj7
C13♯11
Amaj7
N
G♯ locrian
Gmaj7♭5
O
Fmaj7♭5
E♭maj7♭5
P
F♯maj7
E♭maj7
Emaj7
D♭maj7
Dmaj7
Bmaj7
C13♯11
Amaj7
Q
G♯ locrian
8va
Gmaj7♭5

R
Fmaj7♭5
E♭maj7♭5
S
F♯maj7
E♭maj7
Emaj7
D♭maj7
Dmaj7
Bmaj7
C13♯11
Amaj7
T
G♯ locrian
8va
Gmaj7♭5
(8va)
U
Fmaj7♭5
(8va)
E♭maj7♭5
V
F♯maj7
E♭maj7
Emaj7
D♭maj7

Dmaj7
Bmaj7
C13♯11
Amaj7
W
G♯ locrian
Gmaj7♭5
X
Fmaj7♭5
3
3
3
3
3
3
E♭maj7♭5
Y
F♯maj7
E♭maj7
Emaj7
D♭maj7
Dmaj7
Z
Bmaj7
C13♯11
Amaj7
G♯ locrian
Gmaj7♭5
3

11
11
11
AA
Fmaj7♭5
3
3
6
6
E♭maj7♭5
3
BB
F♯maj7
E♭maj7
Emaj7
D♭maj7
3
Dmaj7
Bmaj7
C13♯11
CC
Piano Solo
Amaj7
G♯ locrian
DD
Drum Solo
Gmaj7♭5
139
88
EE
Sax Solo
G♯ locrian
Gmaj7♭5

FF
Fmaj7♭5
E♭maj7♭5
GG
F♯maj7
E♭maj7
Emaj7
D♭maj7
Dmaj7
Bmaj7
C13♯11
HH
Amaj7
G♯ locrian
Gmaj7♭5
II
Fmaj7♭5
E♭maj7♭5
JJ
F♯maj7
E♭maj7

Emaj7
D♭maj7
Dmaj7
Bmaj7
KK
C13♯11
Amaj7
G♯ locrian
Gmaj7♭5
LL
Fmaj7♭5
E♭maj7♭5
MM
F♯maj7
E♭maj7
Emaj7
D♭maj7
Dmaj7
Bmaj7
C13♯11
Amaj7

NN
Head
G♯m7♭5
Gmaj7♯11
OO
Fmaj7♯11
Emaj7♯11
Fmaj7♯11
E♭sus
Esus4
B♭sus2/A
E♭maj7♯11
3
D/E♭
PP
G♭maj7♭5
E♭maj9
3
1.
Emaj9
D♭maj9
Dmaj13♯11
3
Bmaj9
Gm(maj7)
3
Amaj9
2.
Emaj9
D♭maj9
Dmaj13♯11
3
Bmaj9
C13♯11
3
Amaj9
Emaj13
C♯
D
B
D6/C
Amaj7

Jam for Bobbie

(Benny Golson's solo)

from *Benny Golson: Gone with Golson*

By Benny Golson

Tenor Saxophone

C6
N.C./G
C
C7
F7
C/G
3
A7♭9
Dm7
G7♯5(♭9)
C6
N.C./G
D
C7
F7
C/G
A7♭9
3
Dm7
G7♯5(♭9)
3
3
C6
N.C./G
E
C7

F7
C/G
A7♭9
Dm7
G7♯5(♭9)
C6
N.C./G
F
C7
F7
C/G
A7♭9
Dm7
G7♯5(♭9)
C6
N.C./G
G
C7
F7
C/G
A7♭9
Dm7

G7♯5(♭9)
C6
N.C./G
H
C7
F7
C/G
A7♭9
Dm7
G7♯5(♭9)
C6
N.C./G
I
C7
F7
C/G
A7♭9
Dm7
G7♯5(♭9)
C6
N.C./G

J
C7
F7
C/G
A7♭9
Dm7
G7♯5(♭9)
C6
N.C./G
K
C7
F7
C/G
A7♭9
Dm7
G7♯5(♭9)
C6
N.C./G
L
C7
F7

C/G
A7♭9
Dm7
G7♯5(♭9)
C6
N.C./G
M
C7
F7
C/G
A7♭9
Dm7
G7♯5(♭9)
3
C6
N.C./G
N
C7
F7
C/G
A7♭9
8va
Dm7
G7♯5(♭9)
3

C6
N.C./G
O
C7
F7
C/G
A7♭9
Dm7
G7♯5(♭9)
C6
N.C./G
P
C7
F7
8va
C/G
A7♭9
Dm7
G7♯5(♭9)
C6
N.C./G
Q
C
R Trombone Solo
8
12

12
12
12
12
12
12
12
12
12
12
S Trading 4's with Trombone
C7
F7
3
Dm7
G7#5(b9)
C6
N.C./G
T C7
2
F7
C/G
A7b9
4
U C7
F7
3
Dm7
G7#5(b9)

C6
N.C./G
V
C7
3
F7
C/G
A7♭9
Dm7
3
W
C7
8va
3
3
3
F7
3
Dm7
3
3
G7♯5(♭9)
3
3
3
3
C6
3
3
3
3
N.C./G
3
3
X
C7
3
F7
C/G
A7♭9
Dm7
Y
Bass Solo
3
12
12
12
12

Z Trading 4's (Trombone/ Drums/ Sax/ Drums)
7
Dm7
G7♯5(♭9)
C6
N.C./G
AA
C7
11
C7
F7
7
BB
4
F7
C/G
A7♭9
Dm7
3
CC Head
C7
F6
F♯dim7
C/G
C7
F7
F♯dim7
C/G
C/F
Em7♭5
A7♭9
Dm7
Dm7/G
B
C6
1.
N.C./G
2.
C6
C7♯9

Just One of Those Things

(Hank Mobley's solo)

from *The Jazz Messengers at the Cafe Bohemia*

Words and Music by Cole Porter

D
Em7
F♯m7♭5
B7
Em7
E♭m7
Dm7
G7
C
F7
Bm7
E7
Am7
D7
G
E
Trumpet Solo
4
192
F
Sax Solo
Em7
F♯m7♭5
B7
Em7
E♭m7
Dm7
G7
C
F7
Bm7
E7
Am7
D7
G
F♯m7♭5
B7
G
Em7
F♯m7♭5
B7
Em7
E♭m7
Dm7
G7
C
F7
3
Bm7
E7
Am7
D7
G
3
Gm7
C7

H
Fmaj7
Gm7
C7
F
Em7
A7
D
B7
G♯m7♭5
C♯7
Gm7
C7
F♯m7
B7
Em7
A7
D
F♯m7♭5
B7
I
Em7
F♯m7♭5
B7
Em7
E♭m7
Dm7
G7
C
F7
Bm7
E7
Am7
D7
G
Am7
A♯dim
G
F♯m7♭5
B7
J
Em7
F♯m7♭5
B7
Em7
E♭m7
Dm7
G7
C
F7

Bm7 E7 Am7 D7
G F♯m7♭5 B7
K
Em7 F♯m7♭5 B7
3 3
Em7 E♭m7 Dm7 G7 C F7
Bm7 E7 Am7 D7
G Gm7 C7
L
Fmaj7 Gm7 C7
F Em7 A7
D B7 G♯m7♭5 C♯7 Gm7 C7
F♯m7 B7 Em7 A7 D F♯m7♭5 B7
3 3

M
Em7
F♯m7♭5
B7
Em7
E♭m7
Dm7
G7
C
F7
Bm7
E7
Am7
D7
G
Am7
A♯dim
G
F♯m7♭5
B7
N
Em7
F♯m7♭5
B7
Em7
E♭m7
Dm7
G7
C
F7
Bm7
E7
Am7
D7
G
F♯m7♭5
B7
O
Em7
F♯m7♭5
B7
Em7
E♭m7
Dm7
G7
C
F7

Bm7
E7
Am7
D7
G
Gm7
C7
P
Fmaj7
Gm7
C7
F
Em7
A7
D
B7
G♯m7♭5
C♯7
Gm7
C7
F♯m7
B7
Em7
A7
D
F♯m7♭5
B7
Q
Em7
F♯m7♭5
B7
Em7
E♭m7
Dm7
G7
C
F7
Bm7
E7
Am7
D7
G
Am7
A♯dim
G
F♯m7♭5
B7

R
Em7
F♯m7♭5
B7
Em7
E♭m7
Dm7
G7
C
F7
Bm7
E7
Am7
D7
G
F♯m7♭5
B7
S
Em7
F♯m7♭5
B7
Em7
E♭m7
Dm7
G7
C
F7
Bm7
E7
Am7
D7
G
Gm7
C7
T
Fmaj7
Gm7
C7
F
Em7
A7

D
B7
G♯m7♭5
C♯7
Gm7
C7
F♯m7
B7
Em7
A7
D
F♯m7♭5
B7
U
Em7
F♯m7♭5
B7
Em7
E♭m7
Dm7
G7
C
F7
Bm7
E7
Am7
D7
G
Am7
A♯dim
G
F♯m7♭5
B7
V
Em7
F♯m7♭5
B7
Em7
E♭m7
Dm7
G7
C
F7
Bm7
E7
Am7
D7
G
F♯m7♭5
B7
W
Em7

F♯m7♭5 B7 Em7 E♭m7
Dm7 G7 C F7 Bm7
E7 Am7 D7 G
X
Gm7 C7 Fmaj7
Gm7 C7 F Em7
A7 D B7 G♯m7♭5 C♯7
Gm7 C7 F♯m7 B7 Em7 A7 D F♯m7♭5 B7
Y
Em7 F♯m7♭5 B7
Em7 E♭m7 Dm7 G7 C F7
Bm7 E7 Am7 D7

G
Am7
A♯dim
G
F♯m7♭5
B7
Z
Piano Solo
Em7
127
AA
Trade phrases
(Trumpet)
8
(Drums)
8
BB
Em7
(Tenor)
F♯m7♭5
B7
Em7
E♭m7
Dm7
G7
C
Cm6
Bm7
E7
Am7
D7
G
Gm7
C7
CC
(Drums)
Fmaj7
7
(Trumpet)
8
DD
Head (2nd half)
(Tenor)
Em7
F♯m7♭5
B7
Em7
E♭m7
Dm7
G7
C
Cm6
Bm7
E7
Am7
D7
G
rit.

Lester Leaps In

(Lester Young's solo)

from *Count Basie: The Essential Count Basie Vol. II*

By Lester Young

Tenor Saxophone

Bright Swing (♩ = 246)

A Head

3

G7 G7♯5 C C7/E F G7

C G7 C C7/E F G7

C 1. G7 2. B 7

C

G9 C C7/E F G7 C

Dm7 G7 C C7/E F G7 C

D Solo

G7♭9 C C7/E F F♯dim7 C/G E♭dim7

h.t.

Dm7 G7 C C7/E F F♯dim7 C/G

G7 C C7/E F F♯dim7 C/G E♭dim7

Dm7
G7♯5
C6
C7/E
F
F♯dim7
C
G7
E
C
E7
A7
3
D7♭9
G7
F
C13
C7♯5/E
F6
F♯dim7
C/G
E♭dim7
Dm7
G7♯5
C
C7♯5/E
F6
F♯dim7
C/G
G7♭9
Stop-time
G Sax Solo
C
C/E
E♭dim7
Dm7
C6
C7/E
F
Fm
C
G7
C
3
3

H
E7
A7
D7
G7
I
C
C6
C
J
3
Dm7
G7♯5
C
C7/E
F
F♯dim7
C/G
(Lip down)
C
G7
3
Dm7
G7
C
C7/E
F
F♯dim7
C/G
G7
C
K
4
D7
G7♯5
L
C

3
C
C7/E
F
F♯dim7
C6
M
2
C/G
E♭m
Dm
G7
G7♯5
C
Am7
F
G9
C
C7♯5/E
7
N
8
O
C
C7/E
F
F♯dim7
C/G
C/E
E♭dim7
Dm7
G7
C
G7
P
C
C7/E
F
F♯dim7
C/G
5
8
Q
C
C7/E
F
F♯dim7
C/G
E♭dim7
Dm7
G7♯5
C
G7♯5
C6

Lover Man

(Oh, Where Can You Be?)
(Jackie McClean's solo)
from *Presenting...Jackie McLean*
Words and Music by Jimmy Davis, Roger Ramirez and Jimmy Sherman

*Originally performed on Alto Saxophone.

C
G
Bm7
E7
Bm7
E7
Amaj7
Bm7
C♯m7
Bm7
Amaj7
Am7
D7
Am7
D7
Gmaj7
F♯m7♭5
B7
D
Em7
A7
Em7
A7
Am7
D7
Am7
D7
Gm6
C7
B♭m7
E♭7
Am7
D7
G
F♯m7♭5
B7
E
Sax Solo
Em7
A7

Em7
A7
Am7
D7
Am7
D7
Gm6
C7
B♭m7
E♭7
Am7
D7
G
F♯m7♭5
B7
F
Em7
A7
Em7
A7
Am7
D7
Am7
D7
Gm6
C7
B♭m7
E♭7
Am7
D7
G
G
Bm7
E7
Bm7
E7

Amaj7 Dmaj7 C♯m7 Bm7 Amaj7 Am7 D7
Am7 D7 Gmaj7
F♯m7♭5 B7
H
Em7 A7
Em7 A7 Am7 D7 Am7 D7
Gm6 C7 B♭m7 E♭7 Am7 D7
G
I
Piano Solo
7
J
8
K
Head (2nd half)
Bm7 E7 Bm7 E7
Amaj7 Bm7 C♯m7 Bm7 Amaj7
Am7 D7

Am7
D7
Gmaj7
F♯m7♭5
B7
L
Em7
A7
Em7
A7
Am7
D7
Am7
D7
Gm6
C7
Freely
B♭m7
E♭7
Am7
(Cadenza)
D7♭9
Gmaj7♯11

Lulu's Back in Town

(Branford Marsalis' solo)
from *Ellis & Branford Marsalis: Loved Ones*
Words by Al Dubin
Music by Harry Warren

Tenor Saxophone

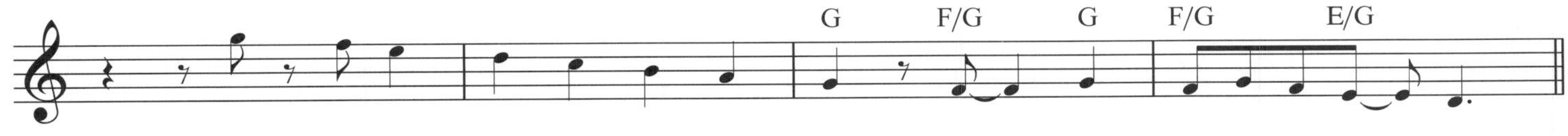

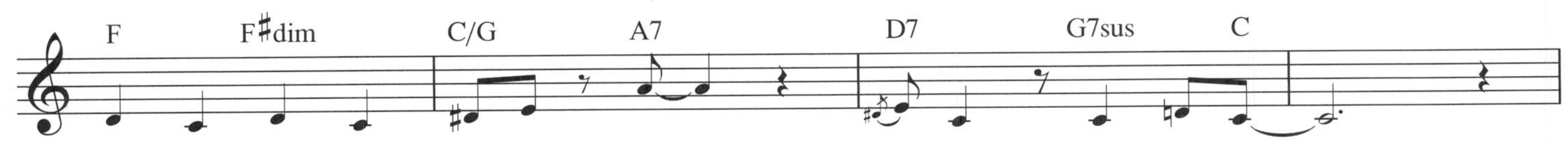

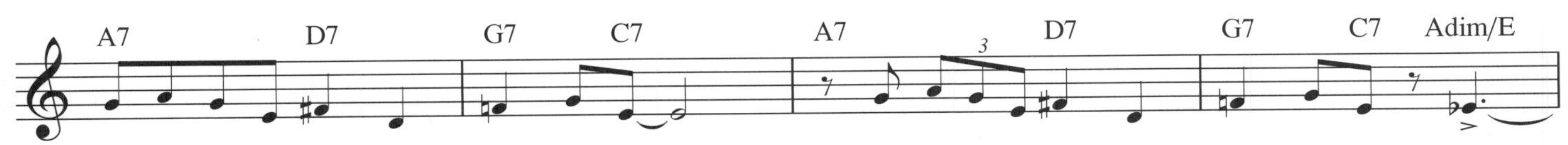

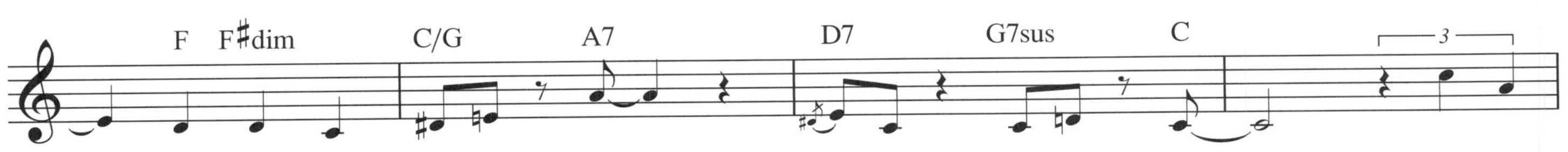

F♯7♭5(♯9) B7♯5 Em7 A7 D9 N.C./G
C
A7 D7 G7 C7 A7 D7 G7 C7 Adim/E
F F♯dim C/G A7 D7 G7sus D♭maj9
8va
D Sax Solo
A7 D7 G7 C7 A7 D7
G7 C7 F7 F♯dim7 C/G A7
D7 G7sus C A7 D7
G7 C7 A7 D7 G7 C
F F♯dim C/G A7 D7 G7sus C
E
F F♯dim7 C/G

F
F♯dim7
C/G
F♯m7
B7♯5
Em7
A7
D9
G7
F
A7
D7
G7
C7
A7
D7
G7
C
F
F♯dim7
C/G
A7
D7
G7sus
D♭maj9
G
A7
D7
G7
C7
A7
D7
G7
C7
F7
F♯dim7
C/G
A7
D7
G7sus
C
A7
D7

G7 C7 A7 D7 G7 C7
F F♯dim C/G A7 D7 G7
C H F F♯dim7
C/G F F♯dim7 C/G
F♯m7 B7♯5 Em7 A7 D9
G7 I A7 D7 G7 C7 A7 D7
G7 C7 Adim/E F F♯dim7 C/G A7
D7 G7sus D♭maj9
J
Piano Solo
A7 D7
32

K
Head
Piano:
A7
D7
G7
C7
A7
D7
G7
C7
Adim/E
F
F♯dim
C/G
A7
D7
G7sus
C
A7
D7
G7
C7
A7
D7
G7
C7
F
F♯dim
C/G
A7
D7
G7sus
C
L
F
Cmaj7
F
Cmaj7
F♯7♭5(♯9)
B7♯5(♯9)
Em7
A7
D9
C/G
Fm(maj7F♯dim
G7
M
A7
D7
G7
C7
A7
D7
G7
C7
F
F♯dim
C/G
A7
D7
F/G
C6
A7♭5(♯9)
Sax:
D7
F/G
C6
A13♭5(♯9)
D7
F/G
N.C.
C7

Luck Be a Lady
(Ken Peplowski's solo)
from *Ken Peplowski: A Good Reed*
By Frank Loesser

D
Gm7/D
B
Ebmaj7
Dmaj7#5/C#
Ebmaj7
E13
Ebmaj7
Dmaj7#5/C#
Ebmaj7
E13
Ebmaj7
Db13
C7b13
Fm7b5
Bb7b9
Ebmaj7
Dmaj7#5/C#
Ebmaj7
F#m7
B7
C
Swing
Emaj7
F#m7
G#m7
A13
D9
C#m7
F#7
E7
D7
C7
Bm
Bm(maj7)
Bm7
G#m7b5
C#7#9
F#m7
Fdim
Em7
A7b13
D
Latin
Dmaj7
Gm7/D
Dmaj7
Gm7/D
Dmaj7
Gm7/D
Dmaj7
Gm7/D
Dmaj7
Em7

F♯m7
Gm
D/F♯
3
3
E
Sax Solo
Dmaj7
Gm7/D
D
E♭7
D
E♭7
D
E♭7
3
D
E♭7
D
E♭7
D
E♭7
D
3
3
3
3
3
3
3
E♭7
D
E♭7
D
3
3
3
3
3
3
F
E♭maj7
E13
3
E♭maj7
Dmaj7♯5/C♯
E♭maj7
E13
E♭maj7
Dmaj7♯5/C♯
E♭maj7
D♭7
C7♭13
B7
B♭7
3
3
3
3
E♭maj7
Dmaj7♯5/C♯
E♭maj7

G
Swing
F♯m7
B7
Emaj7
F♯m7
3
G♯m7
A13
D9
C♯m7
3
F♯7
E7
D7
C7
Bm
3
Bm(maj7)
Bm7
G♯m7♭5
C♯7♯9
F♯m7
Fdim
Em7
A7♭13
H
Dmaj7
Gm7/D
Dmaj7
Gm7/D
Dmaj7
Gm7/D
Dmaj7
Gm7/D
Dmaj7
Em7
F♯m7
Gm
F♯m7
F7
Em7
E♭7
D
3
3
3
I
Latin
A7
D
E♭7
D

E♭7 D E♭7
D E♭7 D E♭7
D E♭7 D E♭7
D E♭7 D
J
E♭maj7
E13 E♭maj7 Dmaj7♯5/C♯
E♭maj7 E13 E♭maj7
Dmaj7♯5/C♯ E♭maj7 D♭13
C7♭13 B7 B♭7 E♭maj7
Dmaj7♯5/C♯ E♭maj7 F♯m7 B7
K
Swing
Emaj7
F♯m7 G♯m7 A13 D9

C♯m7
F♯7
E7
D7
C7
Bm
Bm(maj7)
Bm7
G♯m7♭5
C♯7♯9
F♯m7
Fdim
Em7
A7♭13
L
Dmaj7
Gm7/D
Dmaj7
Gm7/D
Dmaj7
Gm7/D
Dmaj7
Gm7/D
Dmaj7
Em7
F♯m7
Gm
F♯m7
F7
Em7
E♭7
D
A7
M
Latin
Piano Solo
D
63

N
Drum Solo
7
E♭7
(fills)
D
E♭7
D
E♭7
D
2
E♭7
D
O
E♭maj7
E13
E♭maj7
Dmaj7♯5/C♯
E♭maj7
2
Dmaj7♯5/C♯
E♭maj7
D♭13
C7♭13
B7
B♭7
E♭maj7
Dmaj7♯5/C♯
E♭maj7
F♯m7
B7
P
Emaj7
7
Bm
Bm(maj7)
Bm7
G♯m7♭5
C♯7♯9
F♯m7
Fdim
Em7
A7♭13
Q
Dmaj7
14

R
Interlude
A7
N.C.
D
E♭/D
D
E♭/D
4
S
Head
D
E♭/D
D
E♭/D
D
E♭/D
D
Gm7/D
D
Gm7/D
D
Gm7/D
D
Gm7/D
D
Gm7/D
T
E♭maj7
Dmaj7♯5/C♯
E♭maj7
E13
E♭maj7
Dmaj7♯5/C♯
E♭maj7
E13
E♭maj7
D♭13
C7♭13
Fm7♭5
B♭7♭9
E♭maj7
Dmaj7♯5/C♯

U
Swing
Ebmaj7
F#m7
B7
Emaj7
F#m7
G#m7
A13
D9
C#m7
F#7
E7
D7
C7
Bm
Bm(maj7)
Bm7
G#m7b5
C#7#9
F#m7
Fdim
Em7
A7b13
V
Swing
Dmaj7
Gm7/D
Dmaj7
Gm7/D
Dmaj7
Gm7/D
Dmaj7
Gm7/D
Dmaj7
Em7
F#m7
Gm
D/F#
W
Outro
Dmaj7
Ebmaj7
Dmaj7
Ebmaj7
Dmaj7
Ebmaj7
Dmaj7

E♭maj7
Dmaj7
E♭maj7
Dmaj7
E♭maj7
Dmaj7
E♭maj7
Dmaj7
E♭maj7
X
Dmaj7
E♭maj7
Dmaj7
E♭maj7
Dmaj7
E♭maj7
Dmaj7
E♭maj7
Dmaj7
E♭maj7
Dmaj7
E♭maj7
Dmaj7
E♭maj7
Dmaj7
E♭maj7
Y
N.C.
D13
Freely

Mood Indigo

(Johnny Hodges' solo)

from *Jazz 'Round Midnight: The Duke Ellington/Billy Strayhorn Songbook*

Words and Music by Duke Ellington, Irving Mills and Albany Bigard

*Originally performed on Alto Saxophone.

A♭7
G7
D
C7
F
B♭7
C
D7
G7
C
E
Trumpet Solo
16
F
Trombone Solo
16
G
Piano Solo
11
B♭7
Sax Solo (Last 4)
C
D7
G7
C
D.S. al Coda
CODA
Gm
G+
C

My Melancholy Baby

(Lee Konitz's solo)
from *The Real Lee Konitz*
Words by George Norton
Music by Ernie Burnett

*Originally performed on Alto Saxophone.

E
Sax Solo
C
Bb7
A7
Dm7
A7#5
Dm7
F
G7
Bm7
E7
Am7
D7
Dm7
G7
G
C
Bb7
A7
Dm7
A7#5
Dm7
H
Ebdim
C/E
A7
Dm7
G7
C
A7
Dm7
G7
I
C
Bb7
A7
Dm7
A7#5
Dm7

J
G7
Bm7
E7
Am7
D7
Dm7
G7
K
C
B♭7
A7
3
Dm7
A7♯5
Dm7
L
E♭dim
C/E
A7
Dm7
G7
C
A7
Dm7
G7
M
C
B♭7
A7
Dm7
A7♯5
Dm7
3
N
G7
Bm7
E7
Am7
D7
Dm7
G7
3

O
C
B♭7
A7
3
Dm7
A7♯5
Dm7
P
E♭dim
C/E
A7
Dm7
G7
C
A7
Dm7
G7
Q
C
B♭7
A7
Dm7
A7♯5
Dm7
R
3
G7
3
Bm7
E7
Am7
D7
Dm7
G7
S
C
B♭7
A7
Dm7
A7♯5
Dm7

T
E♭dim
C/E
A7
Dm7
G7
C
A7
Dm7
G7
U
C
B♭7
A7
3
Dm7
A7♯5
Dm7
V
G7
Bm7
E7
Am7
D7
Dm7
G7
W
C
B♭7
A7
3
Dm7
A7♯5
Dm7
3
X
(Fadeout begins)
E♭dim
C/E
A7
Dm7
G7
C
A7
(Fadeout complete)
Dm7
G7

Oleo

(Sonny Rollins' solo)

from *Miles Davis: Bag's Groove*

By Sonny Rollins

Tenor Saxophone

D Sax Solo
C
A7
Dm7
E♭dim7
Em7
A7
Dm7
G7
C
F7
3
F
F♯dim7
C/G
A7
Dm7
G7
C7
F
Fm7
C
G7
C
E
E7
A7
D7
2
G7♯9
C
Dm7
G7
C
A7
Dm7
G7
C7
C7/B♭
F/A
F7
C
F
C
F7
G7
Em7
A7
Dm7
G7
C7

F F♯dim7 C/G A7 Dm7 G7
C A7 Dm7 G7 Em7 A7 Dm7 G7
C F G7 C
G
E9 E7♯9 A7sus A7
D7 Dm7/G
G13♯9 C Dm7 G7
Em7 A7 Dm7 G7 3 C C7
F F♯dim7 C/G A7 Dm7 G7
H
C
Piano Solo
63
I
Trumpet Solo
32
D.C. al Fine

My One and Only Love

(Michael Brecker's solo)
from *Michael Brecker*
Words by Robert Mellin
Music by Guy Wood

Slowly, freely
A
Head (alone)
B

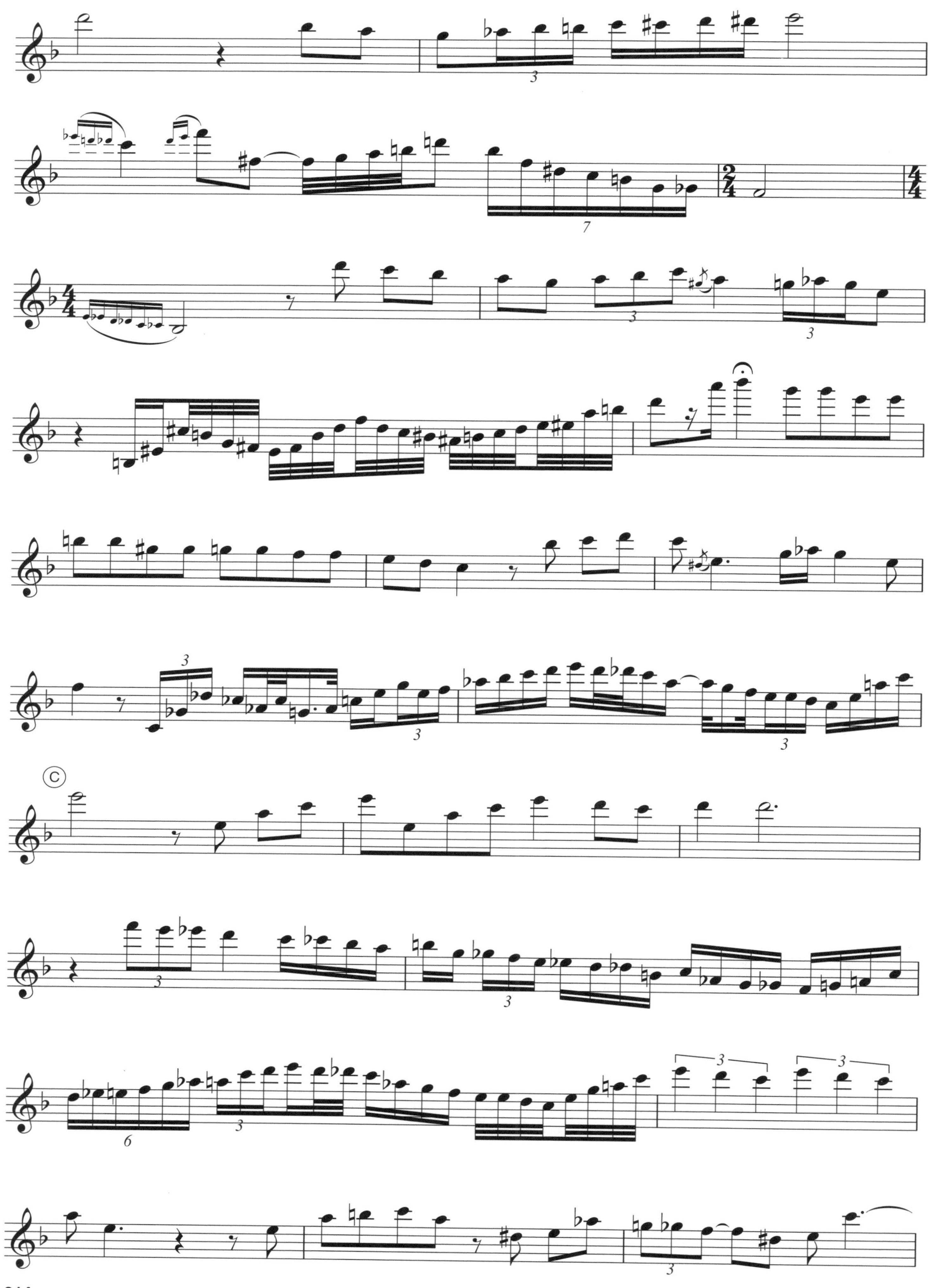
C

D

Moderately slow, steadily (𝅗𝅥 = 60)
E
Head (with ensemble)
F
Dm7
Gm7
C7
C♯dim
Dm7
Cm7
B♭maj7
Am7
D7
Gm7
Em7♭5
A7♯9(♭13)
Dm7
G7
Gm7
C7
Am7
D7
F
Gm7
C7
F
Dm7
Gm7
C7
C♯dim
Dm7
Cm7
B♭maj7
Am7
D7
Gm7
Em7♭5
A7♯9(♭13)
Dm7

G7
Gm7
C7
F
Bm7♭5
E7
G
Am
Bm7♭5
E7♯9(♭13)
Am
C7
Bm7♭5
E7♯9(♭13)
Am
Am(maj7)
Am7
D7
Gm7
D7
Gm7
C♯m7
F♯7
H
F
Dm7
Gm7
C7
C♯dim
Dm7
Cm7
B♭maj7
Am7

D7
Gm7
Em7♭5
A7♯9(♭13)
Dm7
G7
Gm7
C7
F
Gm7
C7
I
Guitar Solo
F
62
Bm7♭5
E7
J
Head (2nd half)
Am
Bm7♭5
E7♯9(♭13)
Am
C7
Bm7♭5
E7♯9(♭13)
Am
Am(maj7)
Am7
D7
Gm7
D7
Gm7
C♯m7
F♯7

K
F
Dm7
Gm7
C7
C♯dim
Dm7
Cm7
B♭maj7
Am7
D7
Gm7
Em7♭5
A7♯9(♭13)
Dm7
G7
Gm7
Freely
F♯13
Fmaj9

Oh, Lady Be Good!

(Zoot Sims' solo)

from *Zoot Sims and the Gershwin Brothers*

Music and Lyrics by George Gershwin and Ira Gershwin

A7 C♯m7 F♯7 B7
E7 A7 F♯7 B7 E7
G
A7 D7 A7 C♯m7 F♯7
B7 E7 A7 F♯7 B7 E7
H
A7 D7 A7 C♯m7 F♯7
B7 E7 A A7
I
D D♯dim A/E A
B7 E7
J
A7 D7 A7 C♯m7 F♯7
B7 E7 A7 F♯7 B7 E7

K
A7 D7 A7 C♯m7 F♯7
B7 E7 A7 F♯7 B7 E7
L
A7 D7 A7 C♯m7 F♯7
B7 E7 A A7
M
D D♯dim A/E A
B7 E7
N
A7 D7 A7 C♯m7 F♯7
B7 E7 A7 F♯7 B7 E7
O
A7 D7 A7 C♯m7 F♯7
B7 E7 A7 F♯7 B7 E7

P
A7 D7 A7 C#m7 F#7
B7 E7 A
Q
A7 D D#dim A/E
A B7
R
E7 A7 D7
A7 C#m7 F#7 B7 E7
S
Outro (Fadeout)
A7 F#7 B7 E7 A7 F#7 B7 E7
A7 F#7 B7 E7 A7 F#7 B7 E7
A7 F#7 B7 E7 A7 F#7 B7 E7
(Fadeout complete)
A7 F#7 B7 E7 A7 F#7 B7 E7

On a Slow Boat to China

(Sonny Stitt's solo)

from *Sonny Stitt: A Little Bit of Stitt*

By Frank Loesser

E
Sax Solo
C
Dm7
G7
C
Am7
Dm7
D♯dim
C
Bm7
E7
F
Edim
Dm7
F
D♯dim
C
B♭7
A7
D7
Dm7
G7
G
C
Em7
A7
Dm
D♯dim
C
Bm7
E7
F
Edim
Dm7
H
F
B♭7
Bdim
C
Em7♭5
A7♭9
Dm7
G7
C
Dm7
G7
I
Piano Solo
C
30
Dm7
G7

J
Head
C Am7 Dm7 D♯dim C
Bm7 E7 F Edim Dm7
K
D♯dim C B♭7
A7 D7
Dm7
G7
L
C Em7 A7 Dm
D♯dim C Bm7 E7 F Edim Dm7
M
F B♭7 Bdim C Em7♭5 A7♭9
Tag
Dm7 G7 Em7♭5 A7 Dm7
G9sus G13♭9 C C13♭9

Quiet Nights of Quiet Stars

(Corcovado)

(Stan Getz's solo)

from *Stan Getz with Laurindo Almeida*

English Words by Gene Lees

Original Words and Music by Antonio Carlos Jobim

Tenor Saxophone

Bossa (♩ = 144)

Intro-Bass

3

A Head

E9

B♭dim7 A7 Lay Back D7sus A♭ A♭/D

Gmaj7 Gm7 3 C9

Dmaj6/9 3 B7♯5(♭9) 3 E13 3

B

Gm6 Gm6/E Gdim7 Bm7 E9

B♭dim7 Lay Back Am7 D7sus

Gmaj7 Gm F♯m7

Bm7 Em7 A13♭9 3 6

Am6 Am6/C 6 B7♯5(♭9)♯11 Em7 A7sus

C Chorus-Guitar Solo
Dmaj6/9
E9
35
Sax Solo
E13
D
B♭dim7
Delay
Am7
D7sus♭9
A♭maj7
D7
Gmaj6/9
Gm7
C7
Dmaj6/9
B7♯5(♭9)
E13
Gm6
Em7
Bm
Bm/F♯
E
E13
B♭dim7
Am7
D7♭9
Gmaj7
Gm7
F♯m7
Bm7
Em7
A13♭9
F♯m7♭5/A
F♯m7♭5/C
B7♭9(♯11)
Em7
A13♭9

F
Dmaj6/9
E13
Piano Solo
35
G
Head
E9
B♭dim7
Am7
D7sus
A♭
Gmaj7
Gm7
Dmaj7
B7♯5(♭9)
E9
Gm6
Gdim7
Bm7
H
E13
B♭dim7
Am7
D7sus
Gmaj7
Gm
F♯m7
Bm7
Em7
A13♭9
Am6
Am6/C
B7♯9(♯11)
Em7
A7sus♭9
A7♭9
Dmaj6/9

Ramblin'

(Ornette Coleman's solo)

from *Ornette Coleman: Change of the Century*

By Ornette Coleman

*Originally performed on Alto Saxophone.

E
A
E
B
E
D
3
3
A
E
A
B
E
E
A
E
A
E
B
E
F

A
E
B
E
G
A
E
A
E
B
E
H
A
E
B
E
I
A

E
A
E
B
E
J
A
E
B
E
K
Trumpet Solo
52
Bass Solo
47
L
Head
3
3
M
Head 2nd time

3
3
N
Fills
3
3
O
Ending
5

St. Thomas

(Sonny Rollins' solo)

from *Sonny Rollins: Saxophone Colossus*

By Sonny Rollins

Tenor Saxophone

Calypso (𝅗𝅥 = 208)

16

(A) **Head**

N.C. A9♯5

Dmaj9 F♯m7 B7♭9 Em7 A7 D

F♯m7♭5 C7 B7 Em7 B♭7 A7

D7 F♯7 G G♯dim7 D/A A7♭9♯11 D

(B)

D6/9 A7♯11 D A7

D F♯m7 B7 Em7 A7♯11 D

F♯m7♭5 B7 Em7 B♭7 A7

D7 D7/F♯ G G♯dim7 D/A A7♭9♯11 D

C Sax Solo
D9 F♯m7♭5 B13♯11 Em11 A7♯11 D E♭7
D F♯m7♭5 B7 Em7 A13 D6 A9♯5
F♯m7♭5 B7♭9 Em7 B♭7♯5 A7 A13 A7♭9♯5
D9 D13/F♯ G G♯dim7 D/A A7♭9♯11 D
D
D6/9 Fm7♭5 B7♭9 Em7 A13 Dmaj9 A7
D6/9 F♯m11♭5 B13♭9♯11 Em11 A13♭9
3
D F♯m7♭5 B7
3
Em7 B♭13♭9 A13♭9 D D7/F♯
3 3
G G♯dim7 D/A A13 D6/9 A9♯5

E
D6/9
B9
Em7
A13♭9
D6/9
A13♭9
D6
B7♭9♯11
Em7
A13♭9
D6/9
F♯m7♭5
B7
Em7♭5
A7
A13
A7♭9♯5
D7
G
G♯dim7
D6/9/A
A7♭9♯11
D
F
D6/9
F♯m7
B7♭9
Em7
A9♯5
D6/9
A13♭9
D6/9
B7♯11
Em11
A7
Dmaj9
F♯m7♭5
B7♯9
Em7♭5
A7♯9♯5
D9
D7/F♯
G
G♯dim7
D/A
D
A9♯5
G
D6/9
B7♭9

Em7
A7
D6
A13♭9
D6/9
B7♭9
Em7
A13♭9
D6/9
A7♭9
D9
3
3
B7♭9♯11
3
Em7♭5
A7♭9♯11
D7
D7/F♯
G
3
G♯dim7
D/A
A7sus♭9
D
A7♭9♯11
H
D
3
Drum Solo
79
I
Sax Solo
D
Em7
F♯m7
B7♯11
Em7
A7♭9♯5
D6/9
A13♭9
D6/9
F♯m7
B7
Em7
A7♭9♯11
D6/9
F♯m7♭5
B7♭9♯5

Em7
A7♭9♯5
D9
G6
G♯dim7
D/A
A7♭9♯11
D6/9
J
D6/9
B13♭9
Em7
A13♭9♯11
Dmaj9
D6/9
Bdim7
Em11
A9♯5
D6/9
F♯m11♭5
B7♯9♯5
Em11♭5
A7♭9♯11
A13♭9
D6
G6
G♯dim7
D/A
A7♯5
D6/9
A7♯9
K
D6/9
B7♭9♯5
Em9
A13
A7♭9♯5
D6/9
B13♭9
Em7
A7♯9♯5
D6/9

F♯m7♭5
B7♭9♯5
Em7♭5
A7♯9♯5
D6
D7/F♯
G
G♯dim7
A13sus
A7♭9♯11
A13♭9
D6/9
A9♯5
L
D9/A
C/G
F♯m7♭5
B7♭9♯5
Em7
A13♭9
D6/9
A13♭9
D6/9
B7♭9♯5
Em7
A7♭9♯11
D6/9
A9♯5
F♯m7♭5
B13♭9
Growl
Em7♭5
A7♯9♯5
D6
D7♯11/F♯
G
G♯dim7
D6/A
A7
A9♯5
M
D9
Piano Solo
63

N Head
D6/9
A7♭9♯11 D6
A13
Dmaj9
F♯m7
B7♯5
Em9
A7♯11 D
A9♯5
F♯m7♭5
B7♯9♯5
Em7♭5
A7♯9♯5
D9
D7/F♯
G
G♯dim7
D/A
A9♯5
D6/9
Half-tongue
A13♭9
O
D6/9
B7♭9
A13 D6/9
A13
D6/9
F♯m7
B7♭9
Em11
A13♭9 D6/9
F♯m7♭5
C7
B7
Em7
B♭maj7♯5
A9sus
D7
D7/F♯
G
G♯dim7
D/A
A7♯5
D6/9

Recorda Me

(Joe Henderson's solo)
from *Joe Henderson: Page One*
By Joe Henderson

C Cm7 F7 B♭
B♭m7 E♭7 A♭ Am7 D7
G F♯7♯9(♭13) C Bm13
Dm13
G7
C Cm7 F7
B♭ B♭m7 E♭7
3
A♭ Am7 D7
3
G F♯7♯9(♭13) D Bm13

Dm13
G7
C
Cm7
F7
B♭
B♭m7
E♭7
A♭
Am7
D7
G
F♯7♯9(♭13)
E
Bm13
Dm13
G7
C
Cm7
F7
B♭
B♭m7
E♭7
A♭
Am7
D7
G
F♯7♯9(♭13)

F
Trumpet Solo
Bm13
78
G
Piano Solo
31
F♯7♯9(♭13)
H
(Piano solo continues)
Bm13
Dm13
G7
7
1.
2.
I
Head
Bm13
Dm13
G7
C
Cm7
F7
B♭
B♭m7
E♭7
A♭
Am7
D7
1.
G
F♯7♯9(♭13)
2.
G
F♯7♯9(♭13)

Seven Come Eleven

(Dexter Gordon's solo)

from *Lionel Hampton Presents Dexter Gordon*

By Benny Goodman and Charles Christian

C
F
D
Sax Solo
F Adim B♭ Bdim Am7 D7 Gm7 C7
F Adim B♭ Bdim Am7 D7 Gm7 C7
E
F Adim B♭ Bdim Am7 D7 Gm7 C7
F Adim B♭ Bdim Gm7 C7 F
F
E7 A7
D7 G7 C7

G
F Adim B♭ Bdim Am7 D7 Gm7 C7
F Adim B♭ Bdim Am7 D7 Gm7 C7
H
F Adim B♭ Bdim Am7 D7 Gm7 C7
F Adim B♭ Bdim Am7 D7 Gm7 C7
3
I
F Adim B♭ Bdim Am7 D7 Gm7 C7
F Adim B♭ Bdim Gm7 C7 F
J
E7 A7
D7 G7 C7
K
F Adim B♭ Bdim Am7 D7 Gm7 C7
F Adim B♭ Bdim Am7 D7

L
Gm7 C7 F Adim B♭ Bdim Am7 D7
Gm7 C7 F Adim B♭ Bdim
Am7 D7 Gm7 C7
3
M
F Adim
B♭ Bdim Am7 D7 Gm7 C7 F Adim
B♭ Bdim Gm7 C7 F
N
E7
A7 D7
G7 C7
O
F Adim
B♭ Bdim Am7 D7 Gm7 C7
F Adim B♭ Bdim Am7 D7 Gm7 C7
P
Vibraphone Solo
F
31
Q
32

R
Guitar Solo
32
S
Piano Solo
32
T
Trade 4's with Vibes
4
F
Adim
B♭
Bdim
Am7
D7
Gm7
C7
F
Adim
2
Gm7
C7
F
Adim
B♭
Bdim
Gm7
C7
F
4
D7
3
G7
C7
3
C7
F
Adim
B♭
Bdim
Am7
D7
Gm7
C7
U
4
F
Adim
B♭
Bdim
Am7
D7
Gm7
C7
F
Adim
2
Gm7
C7
F
Adim
B♭
Bdim
Gm7
C7
F
4
D7

G7
C7
4
F
Adim
B♭
Bdim
Am7
D7
Gm7
C7
V
Head (1st half)
(Fadeout begins)
F
(cues: rhythm section in unison)
W
(Fadeout complete)

Take Five

(Paul Desmond's solo)
from *Dave Brubeck Quartet: Time Out*
By Paul Desmond

*Tenor Saxophone

*Originally performed on Alto Saxophone.

Fm Cm7 Fm Cm7
D
Solo
Fm Cm7
Fm Cm7 Fm Cm7 Fm Cm7
Fm Cm7 Fm Cm7 Fm Cm7
Fm Cm7
E
Fm Cm7 Fm Cm7
Fm Cm7 Fm Cm7 Fm Cm7
Fm Cm7 Fm Cm7 Fm Cm7
F
Fm Cm7 Fm Cm7 Fm Cm7
Fm Cm7 Fm Cm7 Fm Cm7
Fm Cm7 Fm Cm7
G
Drum Solo
Fm Cm7
Fm Cm7
87
Fm Cm7

H
Head
Fm
Cm7
Fm
Cm7
Fm
Cm7
3
3
Fm
Cm7
Fm
Cm7
Fm
Cm7
3
Fm
Cm7
Fm
Cm7
I
D♭
G7♭5/D♭
3
Cm
Fm/C
B♭m
E♭7/B♭
A♭
Cm
D♭
G7♭5/D♭
Cm
Fm/C
B♭m
E♭7/B♭
G7♭5
C7
J
Fm
Cm7
Fm
Cm7
3
Fm
Cm7
Fm
Cm7
Fm
Cm7
3
K
Outro
Fm
Cm7
Fm
Cm7
Fm
Cm7
Fm
Cm7
3
3
3
Fm
Cm7
Fm
Cm7
Fm
Cm7
Fm
Cm7
3
3
Fm
Cm7
Fm
Cm7
Fm
Cm7
Fm

What a Little Moonlight Can Do

(Lew Tabackin's solo)

from *Lew Tabackin: What a Little Moonlight Can Do*

Words and Music by Harry Woods

Tenor Saxophone

Fast (𝅗𝅥 = 154)

Intro

C F7

G E7

Am7 D7

Ⓐ

Head

G N.C. 3 G

Bm7 E7 Am

Am7

D7 G

Ⓑ

Dm7 3 G7 Cmaj7

Cm7
G
Bm7
E7
A7
Am
3
E7
Am7
D7
C
G
Bm7
E7
Am
3
Bm7♭5
E7
Am
F♯m7♭5
B7
Em
Dm7
G7
D
Cmaj7
Cm
G
Bm7
E7
Am7

D7
G
E
Sax Solo
Am7
D7
G
Bm7
E7
Am
Am7
D7
G
F
Dm7
G7
Cmaj7
Cm7
G
Bm7
E7
A7
Am
E7
G
Am7
D7
G

Bm7
E7
Am
Bm7♭5
E7
Am
3
F♯m7♭5
B7
Em
3
Dm7
G7
H
Cmaj7
Cm
G
Bm7
E7
Am7
D7
G
Am7
D7
I
G
Bm7
E7
Am
3
Am7

D7
G
Dm7
G7
J
Cmaj7
Cm7
G
Bm7
E7
A7
Am
E7
Am7
D7
K
G
Bm7
E7
Am
Bm7♭5
E7
Am
F♯m7♭5
B7
Em
Dm7
G7

L
Cmaj7
Cm
G
Bm7
E7
Am7
D7
G
Am7
D7
M
Piano Solo
G
63
N
Bass Solo
64
O
Sax Solo
G
Bm7
E7
Am
Am7
D7
G
Dm7
G7
P
Cmaj7

Cm7
G
Bm7
E7
A7
3
Am
E7
Q
Head (2nd half)
Am7
D7
G
Bm7
E7
Am
Bm7♭5
E7
Am
F♯m7♭5
B7
Em
Dm7
G7
R
Cmaj7
Cm
G
Bm7
E7
Am7
D7
G
Dmaj7♯5/G

Turnaround
(Joshua Redman's solo)
from *Joshua Redman: Wish*
By Ornette Coleman

D7
G7
D7
B7
E7
A7
D
Bm7
Em7
A7
D
D7
G7
D7
G7
D7
B7
E7
A7
D
Bm7
E
Em7
A7
D7
G7
D7
G7
D7
B7
E7
A7

F
D
Bm7
Em7
A7
D7
G7
D7
G7
D7
8va
B7
E7
A7
D
Bm7
Em7
A7
G
D7
G7
D7
G7
D7
B7
E7
A7
D
Bm7
Em7
A7
H
D7
G7
D7

G7
D7
B7
E7
A7
D
Bm7
I
Em7
A7
D7
G7
D7
G7
D7
B7
E7
A7
D
Bm7
Em7
A7
J
Guitar Solo
D7
K
Bass Solo
59
47
D.S. al Coda
CODA
D/A
A7
D/A
A7
D/A
A7
C♯5
D5

Undecided

(Lucky Thompson's solo)

from *Lucky Thompson: Complete Parisian Small Group Sessions 1956-1959*

Words by Sid Robin

Music by Charles Shavers

Dm7 G7 C C♯dim Dm7 G7
E
C F7
Dm7 G7 C
F
C7 F
D7 G7
G
C F7
Dm7 G7 C C♯dim Dm7 G7
H
C F7
Dm7 G7 C C♯dim Dm7 G7
I
C F7

Dm7
G7
C
J
C7
F
D7
G7
K
C
F7
Dm7
G7
C
C♯dim
Dm7
G7
L
Guitar Solo
C
15
M
Vibes Solo
16
N
Piano Solo
32
31
Dm7
G7
O
Sax Solo
C
F7
Dm7
G7

P
C
C♯dim
Dm7
G7
C
F7
Dm7
G7
C
Q
C7
F
D7
R
Head (last 8)
G7
G7+
C
F7
Dm7
G7
Tag
C/G
C7/G
Outro
C7

Walk On By

(Stanley Turrentine's solo)

from *Blue Note Plays Bacharach*

Lyric by Hal David

Music by Burt Bacharach

Am
D
Gm7
Am7
Gm7
Am7
Dm
Am
B♭maj7
C7
D
Fmaj7
B♭maj7
Fmaj7
B♭maj7
Fmaj7
B♭maj7
Fmaj7
E
Sax Solo
Am
D
Am
D
Am
D
Gm7
Am7
Gm7
Am7
Dm
Am
B♭maj7
F
C7
Fmaj7

B♭maj7
Fmaj7
B♭maj7
Fmaj7
B♭maj7
Fmaj7
G
Am
D
Am
D
Am
D
Gm7
6
Am7
Gm7
Am7
Dm
Am
B♭maj7
C7
H
Fmaj7
B♭maj7

Fmaj7
B♭maj7
Fmaj7
B♭maj7
Fmaj7
I
Trumpet Solo
Am
19
J
Head
Am
D
Am
D
Am
D
Gm7
Am7
Gm7
Am7
Dm
Am
B♭maj7
C7
K
Fadeout begins
Fmaj7
B♭maj7
Fmaj7
B♭maj7
Fmaj7
B♭maj7
Fmaj7
B♭maj7
Fmaj7
Fadeout ends

Work Song

(Cannonball Adderley's solo)

from *The Cannonball Adderley Quintet - Paris 1960*

By Nat Adderley

*Originally performed on Alto Saxophone.

D ped
C
Gm7
lay back
Tutti
D7
Gm7
E♭7
D7♭9
Gm7
G7
C7
D7
D
Gm7
8va
D7
8va
Gm7
E♭7
D7
Gm7
lay back
8va
Tutti
G7
E♭7
E
D7+
Gm7
D7
Gm7

E♭7
D7♭9
F
G6/9
A7
D7♯9
G7
C7
D7
Gm7
D7
G
Gm6
D7
Gm7
D7
Gm(maj7)
E♭7
H
Gm7
8va
G7
C7

Am7
D7
Gm7
D7
I
Gm7
6
tr
tr
tr
3
8va
3
B♭m7
E♭7
Am7
D7
(8va)
3
J
Gm7
Am7
D7♭9
Gm7
Am7♭5
D7
G7
3
C7
3
E♭7
D7
Gm7
Trumpet Solo (1.–7.)
Piano Solo (8.–13.)
15
1.–12.
13.
D.S. al Coda
Bass cues
CODA
N.C.
Sax
Rim shot
Cornet cues